JUST PEACE
A Revolution in Progress

Compiled by Mary Fritz, CSJ
Edited by Robert Keeler

Published by Pax Christi USA

Just Peace
A Revolution in Progress

Compiled by Mary Fritz, CSJ
Edited by Robert Keeler
Editorial team: Holly Knight; Nancy Small; Mary Ellen
        Cummings, OSB; Lori Swanson Nemenz
Layout and design by Amy L. Kosmack
Cover design by Jodi-Staniunas Hopper
Printed by Printing Technologies
Item No. 525-452

© 2000, Published by Pax Christi USA
532 West Eighth St.
Erie, PA 16502
814.453.4955
info@paxchristiusa.org
www.nonviolence.org/pcusa
ISBN 0-9666285-2-7

CONTENTS

Introduction *by Mary Fritz, CSJ*   4

**The Spiral of Violence: A Framework for
Understanding Aspects of Violence**
Rev. Paul Surlis   10

**Utilizing Just War Teaching to Condemn Modern War: A
Reflection on the Developing Church Teaching**
Rev. Francis X. Meehan   23

The Theology of Peacemaking
Mary Elsbernd, OSF   46

Disturbing The Peace
Ibrahim M. Abdil-Mu'id Ramey   64

The Problem of Peace and Justice in Evolutionary Perspective
Rev. Richard Viladesau   73

Jubilee: A Catechesis for "Being Peace"
Maria Harris   95

The Fall of Babel: O Happy Fault!
Rosemary Luling Haughton   114

Obedience and Vocation: Faithful Resistance
Elizabeth McAlister   124

Appendix: *Modern War and Christian Conscience*   133

INTRODUCTION

In recent years, the public has become increasingly familiar with the phrase "just war," invented by theologians to specify the conditions under which international conflict might be morally permissible. In presenting a collection centered around the theme of "just peace," we hope to "move the question," to advance the conversation between those who believe that war can still be "justified" and those who believe the very expression "just war" is a contradiction in terms.

As we exchange ideas, the hope is that our thinking may evolve toward a new synthesis. We ask the questions: How do we bring peace to an increasingly violent world? How do we ever justify killing to bring about an end to killing? What are the conditions that give rise to violence? How can we work to get at the roots of the injustices that erupt like volcanoes, destroying everything wholesome in their path? In our discussion and dialogue, how can we avoid the pitfalls of all heated arguments: the exchange of slogans and epithets, the lack of respect for other opinions, and, yes, the violence that has characterized some of the exchanges in the pro-life, pro-choice debate?

What is needed and what has, in fact, begun to happen within the "*sensus fidelium*" is a paradigm shift, a movement away from the presumption that war is a viable or moral resolution for conflict. This calls for a renewed creative energy that seeks not only to keep the vision of peace alive, but to render it viable, having its own imperative, its own modality, its own implementation. In other words, we need to learn how to "wage peace" at least as effectively as we've learned (so demonically) to wage war.

The collection begins with the Rev. Paul Surlis. While not focusing specifically on the "just war" discussion, Surlis brings to our conversation the unique viewpoint of liberation theology, so influential in

Latin America. Using an analytical tool called "the spiral of violence," he takes a deeper cut into the question of how and why violence erupts. This tool emerged from the boundary-breaking work of two liberation theologians, the Rev. Gustavo Gutiérrez of Peru and Dom Helder Camara of Brazil. This theory points out that, when violence erupts in a segment of society, it is often because violence already exists in that society in some form of oppression. In the framework of the "spiral," Surlis shows some of the ways in which violence is endemic to our capitalist system. Once again, we are powerfully challenged to get to the root causes of conflict and attempt to be engaged actively in becoming part of the solution, rather than remaining part of the problem.

"Utilizing Just War Teaching to Condemn Modern War: A Reflection on the Developing Church Teaching," by the Rev. Francis X. Meehan brings the perspective of moral theology to the discussion. He suggests that "rather than seek from the church a total repudiation of 'just war' teaching," peace activists "might instead challenge the church to such a rigorous application of 'just war' teaching as to preclude the possibility of justifying any modern war." With clarity, logic and courage, Meehan develops four basic affirmations that lead to a powerful conclusion on the connection between being a eucharistic people and the repudiation of modern warfare.

Relying heavily on scriptural themes, Mary Elsbernd, OSF, professor of social ethics, contributes a chapter, "The Theology of Peace," that calls to mind that the Incarnation has implications not only for Christians but for the whole created universe. She reminds us that Jesus in his person reconciled "opposites," such as earth and heaven or the human and the divine. Guiding us through New Testament revelation, she shows us how Jesus leads us to become who he was, that is: "incarnate love and the good news of reconciliation." She concludes with an incisive caution against taking Jesus' words out of context and

5

using them as "proof texts" for a theology of peacemaking, but rather urges us to base our theology upon the person of Jesus as the reconciliation of God.

In his essay, "Disturbing the Peace," Ibrahim M. Abdil-Muʾid Ramey confronts us with the "false peace" of conformity with evil and injustice. He describes that false peace as the "false nonviolence" that implicitly supports the social status quo in the absence of visible social conflict, the false nonviolence of acquiescence to injustice or oppression undergirded by the belief that social stratification and social privilege are natural states of society. Simply put, says Ramey, "the construction of 'false nonviolence' teaches us nothing more than the passive surrender to permanent oppression."

Ramey divulges his personal struggles with racial oppression to show how the nonviolence of Dr. Martin Luther King Jr., far from being passive resistance, far from perceiving peace as the mere absence of armed conflict, taught him to analyze and measure peace by the immorality and injustice embedded in unexamined social institutions. King's peace, says Ramey, is rooted in abiding and absolute justice. The nonviolence of Martin Luther King Jr., he says, "is a lighthouse that illuminates the struggle for a world that is free of racial injustice, poverty and war. …It disturbs the peace of silent complicity with unjust institutions and actions."

In "The Problem of Peace and Justice in Evolutionary Perspective," the Rev. Richard Viladesau, a student of Bernard Lonergan, moves us into the heart of the argument between absolute pacifism and the "just war theory," with a precision and logic that is masterful and challenging. He suggests that contemporary anthropology and sociobiology point to causes of violence and possible conditions for change. Such a view gives us hope that the moral perspective regarding war may be subject to a kind of evolution. Certain conditions may make possible the emergence of nonviolence as "a universal and realizable moral option." These conditions present a great challenge to peacemakers in terms of working for the justice that is the prerequisite for true peace.

Maria Harris develops the scriptural theme of Jubilee as a catechesis toward "being peace." Harris begins: "My hope is to weave together the Buddhist theme of being peace, the Jewish theme of Jubilee and the Catholic work of peace catechesis espoused by Pax Christi." She weaves these three strands together with great clarity and dexterity as she explores the five demands of the biblical jubilee. Within this framework, Harris gives us grounding in a spirituality of "being peace" and offers many practical guidelines for "living peace" based on justice and forgiveness.

Rosemary Luling Haughton's "The Fall of Babel: O Happy Fault," is a kind of allegory based on the story in Genesis. Profoundly yet simply, she shows how "difference," which creates so much fear and misunderstanding, was meant to be a blessing, not a curse. Writing with bold and broad strokes, she depicts the sources of war: fear of difference, prejudice and greed. In contrast, she describes the wisdom gained by entering into "the other's" experience, language and story. She envisions a time when some will have learned how to live in peace together and will share that wisdom with others. Then the earth will be renewed in the Spirit.

As a conclusion to this thought-provoking and insightful collection, we listen to a different voice: the prophetic and disturbing words of Elizabeth McAlister, long-time peace activist and war resister. She challenges us to move out of our comfortable and safe position on the sidelines, to accept the prophetic call rooted in the seminal grace of our baptism. She argues that we who "do good" but refuse to resist the structural evils in society are responsible for what we fail to do.

McAlister urges us to respond to the prophetic imperative in Acts 4:19 to "obey God rather than humans."

Finally, as an appendix to this body of work, we have included an article that Meehan cites in his essay. Published in 1991 as an editorial in the *La Civiltà Cattolica* (a Rome-based Jesuit publication considered to reflect unofficial Vatican opinion), it is thought to be the strongest statement to date on the evil of modern warfare.

The inspiration for this collection flows from the international peace movement, Pax Christi, as it has developed in this country and, for me, especially on Long Island. Among the priorities of Pax Christi are the disarmament and demilitarization of nations. It also expresses great concern over the sale of arms by the United States to Third World countries and the American expenditure of billions of dollars on defense. The movement's purview includes human rights everywhere and the work of reconciliation among enemies, races and other groups. Pax Christi also focuses on peace education or "catechesis," through books and educational materials, retreats, lectures and so on.

The spirituality of nonviolence and peacemaking is at the heart of all our activity, as we struggle to integrate these values in our way of thinking, speaking and acting. This does not mean passivity, for we have committed ourselves with all our strength to "being peace" in very practical and positive ways. The lifeblood of Pax Christi is the small local group, which meets regularly for prayer, study and action. An energy and excitement, a sense of purpose and mission, characterize these "cells" of peacemaking.

The emergence of this "Peace Church" within the heart of the Catholic Church is an encouraging sign. And the numbers are growing. As some of our authors have indicated, we are in an evolutionary process, in which the very idea of war as a means of resolving human conflict may someday become a curiosity, a museum piece, a dinosaur. If that is to occur, we need not just an evolution, but a revolution— such a revolution as exploded into the streets of Jerusalem when the Holy Spirit transformed a group of men and women from a church in hiding to a church evangelizing and challenging the empire. May that revolutionary spirit come and renew the face of the earth and the church once again. Maranatha!

Mary Fritz, CSJ
Pax Christi Long Island

Mary Fritz is a Sister of St. Joseph of Brentwood Long Island, N.Y. She spent many years teaching and four years as coordinator of a Center for the Poor. Since 1974, she has been involved with developing lay spirituality and in 1985 opened Bethany House of Prayer in the Parish of St. Patrick's in Bayshore. In 1992, in additon to her ministry, she became coordinator of Pax Christi Long Island and completes her duties in 2000. Her previous publications are Take Nothing for the Journey, *Paulist Press 1985, and* Dancing Before the Ark, *Sisters of St. Joseph, Brentwood, N.Y., 1992.*

THE SPIRAL OF VIOLENCE: A FRAMEWORK FOR UNDERSTANDING ASPECTS OF VIOLENCE

By Rev. Paul Surlis

Analysis of violence in the "spiral of violence" framework is one of the contributions that liberation theology has made to theology and religion, as they seek to evaluate violence morally and try to help eliminate its causes and redress its consequences. Liberation theology may be described as "second-order reflection on praxis" in light of the Word of God, where praxis is understood as theory-inspired action directed to social change.

Liberation theology attained international significance in 1968 when its methodology and concepts were employed by the Conference of Latin American Bishops in their second plenary meeting held at Medellin, Colombia, in the aftermath of the Second Vatican Council (1962-1965). This new way of doing theology has spread to Asia, Africa and all over Latin America.

Though liberation theologies are sympathetic to the aspirations toward justice found in liberal thought and practice, they go beyond liberal perspectives in addressing root causes of oppression and in seeking the structural or systemic changes necessary to achieve empowerment and equal access for all. Liberation theologies seek empowerment for all those who are marginalized, not just for a token few, whose emergence from oppression often conceals the plight of the majority and serves to stabilize an unjust status quo even further.

In its initial stages, Latin American liberation theology focused on poverty and related oppressions that flow from it. Black theology of liberation focuses on race as the underlying oppression, but today it includes poverty, marginalization and gender-related oppressions as well.

Liberation movements are not monolithic. Rather, they resemble families where differences exist together with strong similarities. In this respect, feminist theology of liberation includes practitioners whose areas of concern are white, middle-class issues and persons who also address class, poverty and race-related oppressions, together with those that are gender-based. Reflection reveals that oppressions interlock and reinforce each other. Individually they spawn misery, truncated human lives and death. When the three (race, gender, class) coalesce in a particular group, such as poor women and children of color, the evil effects of oppression are intensified.

Consequently, analyses of oppression, for which theology depends on the social sciences, must attend to issues involving race, class and gender in such a way that people do not overlook the sufferings and distresses of the most marginalized, most powerless groups, even as they pay attention to other worthwhile causes.

A concrete example may help to illustrate the significance of this point. During the Senate hearings on Clarence Thomas' nomination to the Supreme Court, the media devoted considerable attention to Anita Hill's allegations of sexual harassment. Undoubtedly the exchanges, grueling as they were at times, contributed to consciousness-raising on the issue of sexual harassment in the workplace, a predominantly feminist concern.

At around the same time as those hearings, a workplace fire claimed the lives of 25 people, of whom 12 were African-American women, and seriously injured another 56 women. They had all been working in a factory in Hamlet, North Carolina, preparing chickens for sale to the grocery trade. The door through which they tried to escape was locked and no key was available, but the factory had never been inspected for violation of safety regulations.

The tragedy in Hamlet was reported briefly in the press, but there was no national attention or outcry similar to what the Clarence Thomas-Anita Hill hearings evoked. Class, coupled with gender and race, rendered these women almost invisible and silent in their exploitation. Their deaths, almost equally invisible, were less an accident than a crime of corporate neglect and government malfeasance.

We have as yet only told part of the story, however. The chicken production business in the United States is spread over an area in the South called "the broiler belt." Here, factories are scattered in a series of relatively small towns. Little alternative work is available for women, who are often single heads-of-household working for poverty-level wages. They are not unionized, and they work in unsanitary and dangerous conditions.

The capitalist owners of these factories have deliberately placed them in small towns where work is scarce. Because the workforce in each enterprise is relatively small, there is little incentive for union-related activities. Because the towns are small, there is not a sufficient population to produce public outrage over working conditions or criminal accidents (as I believe such incidents should be termed). Compounding the tragedy in this instance, the poverty status of the women, who were also women of color, deprived them of the national spotlight that their plight deserved. Jesse Jackson tried to focus national attention on the tragedy, but national feminist leaders were mostly silent.[1]

Common to the principal theologies of liberation is identification with the oppressed in their struggle for justice and recourse to a spiral-of-violence framework in analyzing causes and consequences of violence.[2]

Spiral of Violence

Studies of violence, especially in philosophical and theological writings, often start with analysis of the legitimacy or illegitimacy of violence in revolts or rebellions aimed at achieving social justice and related forms of political liberation.

Frequently, we hear this question: Is violence (or revolt, or rebellion, or the use of force) justified in the pursuit of needed social change? In itself, this is a valid question, but insofar as it assumes that the revolt or rebellion is the first time violence enters the scene, it is mistaken. In situations where revolutions or uprisings take place, the already-existing state of affairs usually contains a variety of interlocking oppressions, produced by various forms of systemic violence that contribute to others, as we shall see.

Where there is widespread poverty, unemployment, underemployment, poor housing, homelessness, disease, illiteracy and unavailability of land, violence already exists in these situations. This violence maims and destroys persons, even if sometimes it does so silently or without overt acts. Such violence is referred to as being institutionalized or systemic. It is kept in place by a combination of economic and political powerlessness. Persons caught in these situations have little or no access to resources, and they are prevented from gaining it by laws, institutions and property regulations that usually favor a relatively small elite who have resources and power far in excess of their needs. All this collectively is referred to as violence number one (Violence #1 — see chart page 14).

Social Pathologies

Conditions such as these, it is disturbing to note, are not peculiar to so-called Third World or newly developing countries. In varying forms and degrees, similar conditions are found in inner cities in

Spiral of Violence

Read from bottom

VIOLENCE #3
MILITARY

GIVES
RISE TO

VIOLENCE #2
REBELLION

GIVES
RISE TO

VIOLENCE #1
INSTITUTIONALIZED BAD HOUSING,
UNEMPLOYMENT, ILLITERACY, POVERTY

England, the United States, Eastern Europe and the former Soviet Union. Any form of social injustice imposed on persons because of gender, age, color or sexual orientation is a form of violence. In this sense, violence is a condition in which we all may be involved, without ever thinking of ourselves as violent. It is much more pervasive in society than is frequently realized. The resulting poverty, unemployment, hunger and disease sometimes drive people to take part in rebellion or guerrilla warfare. This is violence number two (Violence #2).

It must not be assumed that liberation theologians justify armed rebellion or warfare. On the contrary, the majority of them deplore all violence, and they call for peaceful systemic change of unjust conditions at level one, the condition where, we argued, violence is encountered as injustice or oppression in various guises.

Usually, when armed resistance does occur (Violence #2), the response of the state, at the behest of the wealthy and powerful, is to intensify police activity and call in the national guard or the military to quell the rebellion (Violence #3). When successful, the state use of force pushes people back into the original unjust situation that spawned the rebellion in the first place. So, in the absence of significant reform, the process will inevitably start all over again.[3]

It is often pointed out that St. Thomas Aquinas (circa 1225-1274) declared that unjust laws are a form of violence. Our experience with racist or other discriminatory legislation bears that out. Whenever the rights of groups or classes are denied or restricted by unjust laws, a state of violence exists. Thus, violence is much more pervasive in society nationally and globally than we are frequently prepared to admit. Moreover, we who are affluent, privileged and usually white benefit from laws, structures and arrangements, especially economic ones, that keep other persons in poverty and misery. The same system that generates extreme wealth for some and affluence for many also generates poverty for the masses. This system is global today. It is also, in important respects, outside political control.

Driven by the logic of pursuing ever-increasing profits, heads of corporations, who are non-elected and not publicly accountable (except to shareholders or in the event of flagrant crime), transfer jobs to wherever labor and resources are cheapest, wherever there are slack or non-existent environmental laws. In doing so, they cause devastation in communities, leaving them bereft of jobs. Areas from which jobs are taken and where no replacement is found frequently deteriorate. When rent is not paid, housing becomes dilapidated, the hours of service at libraries are curtailed, schools lack adequate equipment and maintenance. Frequently, outbreaks of arson occur at the behest of property owners, who benefit from insurance payments. Then drugs, crime, homelessness and prostitution escalate in the vacuum created by job loss, which is at the very heart of community disintegration.

There is no question of endeavoring to excuse criminal behavior or to suggest that persons unemployed and poor are determined by circumstances to become criminals. In fact, the majority of the poor and unemployed are decent and law-abiding, and major criminality also occurs among the wealthy and in high places. Rather, there is a need to show that street crime and the violence that draws media headlines and scares people does not occur in a social vacuum. Given the circumstances found in inner cities in the United States, the surprise may be not that we have street violence and crime but that we do not have more of it. In order to justify this line of argument, let us consider the following.

Conditions in the United States

Poverty is still rampant in the United States, both in inner cities and in some rural areas, as government statistics show. The U.S. Census Bureau Report on Poverty 1998 indicates that the poverty rate dropped to 12.7 percent in 1998, down from 13.3 percent in 1997. The number of those who are poor dropped to 34.5 million people, down from 35.6 million people in 1997. In 1998 13.5 million children of people under 18 years of age were poor, the first time since 1980 that the child poverty rate was below 20 percent. The poverty rate for blacks remained unchanged between 1997 and 1998. At 26.1 percent, it is said to be at the lowest level since 1959. The poverty rate for Hispanics is down also – 25.6 percent were poor in 1998, down from 27.1 percent in 1997. Among whites not of Hispanic origin, 8.2 percent were poor in 1998, down from 8.6 percent in 1997.

How Poverty Is Estimated

Louis Uchitelle recently reported in *The New York Times* ("Devising New Math to Define Poverty" 10/18/99) that the Census Bureau has begun to revise its definition of what constitutes poverty in the United States. Arriving at a poverty level has always been a somewhat subjective endeavor. The current formula was devised for President Lyndon Johnson and has remained unchanged since 1965 except for adjustments for inflation. The formula is arrived at by taking a minimally adequate food diet and multiplying it by three, the assumption being that all other expenses – such as rent, transportation, clothing, automobile or housing repairs, entertainment and the unavoidable unexpected expenses that crop up – come to less than twice the cost of a barely adequate food budget. The current formula yields a figure of approximately $16,600 for a family of four.

However, some sociologists and economists say that figure is much too low and they put the threshold for a family of four between $21,000 and $28,000. The higher figure, if adopted, would mean that government spending would rise to pay for benefits tied to the poverty level – benefits such as food stamps and Head Start – and would mean encroaching on the budget surplus – something politicians resist.

Adopting revised, higher figures would put 17 percent of the population, or 46 million people, below the poverty line — a figure considerably higher than the 34.5 million as currently estimated.

Economists and others frequently point out that a majority of the jobs created in the past seven or eight years are ones that pay minimum wage rates and it is reported that in seven million families each parent has two jobs. Obviously, working two jobs leaves little opportunity for time – quality or otherwise – with children. Also, large numbers of jobs, including adjunct teaching positions at numerous universities, are part-time, which means they pay close to the minimum wage and do not include health-care benefits or pension funds. Indeed, a majority of these jobs, including part-time jobs at Catholic universities, violate standards of social justice and reduce labor to a commodity – something condemned for over one hundred years in Catholic social teaching.

Unemployment today is at a little over 4 percent. But when one includes part-time workers, students and those who have become discouraged and stopped looking for work, that still yields a figure in the region of 10 million persons. And if recession comes, as inevitably it will, unemployment figures will increase steeply. Studies indicate that when unemployment increases and safety nets are deficient – as they clearly are at present after massive cuts in welfare benefits – then child abuse, alcohol abuse, drug abuse, admission to mental institutions, death from stress-related diseases, homicide and suicide all increase as well.[4]

Again, there is no question of labeling all unemployed persons as criminals or espousing determinism of any sort. Rather, the issue is recognizing the central importance of decent jobs with adequate benefits in people's lives and the social consequences of chronic unemployment or underemployment when prolonged.

Involuntary unemployment diminishes self-esteem and can cause interpersonal tension. It undermines family stability and well-being. It contributes to community deterioration and neglect of housing, which in turn leads to arson and other crimes. Perhaps up to 70 percent of arson crimes are perpetrated by owners of property whose rental income is falling and for whom insurance reimbursement represents gain. Arson for profit is most frequently not perpetrated by individual criminals or sociopaths. Rather, like corporate crime, it involves collusion between criminal elements in legal, law enforcement, real estate, political, banking and other circles. As a form of corporate criminal behavior, however, it is masked from public scrutiny or awareness and hence from public outrage, despite its exceedingly destructive effects in families, communities and social life.[5]

The value of using the spiral-of-violence paradigm or model in trying to understand crime and violence is that it directs us to root causes, structures and systemic issues, without which views of violence may be incomplete, narrowly focused and may involve countermeasures that are punitive or otherwise blame persons who are themselves driven by forces beyond their control. It should be noted that, in the spiral-of-violence approach, the phase referred to as violence number one (Violence #1) in itself is a situation of real violence. This situation is nearly always one of injustice and exploitation—in other words, a situation where issues of jobs are paramount. The passage of NAFTA has produced much discussion concerning "job flight," "job loss," "jobs going overseas," and so on.

Dynamics of Capitalism

One notes here the complete silence (and this is fairly general in the media at present) concerning the capitalist economic system and its direct causal influence on "job flight." Jobs do not go to non-unionized, small, rural locations of their own accord. Similarly, jobs do not pack their suitcases and go overseas. Corporate boards, heads of corporations and other decision makers close factories in the inner cities or suburbs of the United States and they transfer jobs elsewhere in order to make greater profit. There is no mystery to all this: An inexorable law of the capitalist economic system is that the rate of profit must be continuous and ever-increasing.

It is this inescapable logic, and not malice or lack of compassion, that causes the transfer of jobs to areas where labor and resources are cheapest and where environmental regulations are nonexistent or poorly enforced. Loss of well-paying, meaningful jobs is a central dynamic in causing disintegration of communities and family breakdown, together with racial hostility and violence against women. Building more prisons and giving longer sentences for crimes is a superficial, often knee-jerk, response to symptoms, rather than an address to more complex underlying causes. Underlying factors are often planetary and global in nature, having to do with violence against the environment, unavailability of well-paying jobs, illiteracy in the adult population, lack of decent housing, lack of health-care insurance for millions, and distortion of food production through encroachments by agribusiness. All these are forms of violence in themselves, and they help to spawn racism, violence against children and women and other forms of domestic and social violence. These forms of violence are like the tip of an iceberg whose massive bulk is concealed from view.

Politics of Conversion

Ethical and religious appeals for personal conversion and renunciation of violence, which are always necessary and useful, must also be accompanied by unremitting struggles for justice, according to the maxim "if you want peace, work for justice." Working for justice today involves recognizing that injustices that are local and regional—

homelessness, unemployment, or crimes such as a berserk dismissed employee shooting his boss and coworkers, or street mugging or drug-related murder—may be caused by economic forces that are at once regional, national and global in scope and in their effects. What is too little recognized is that the economic and related decisions we are concerned with here are made by actual, flesh-and-blood men (usually it is men) who are not elected and are not accountable to the hordes of people who are hurt by their decisions.

Working for justice means working for a new way for persons to be human together, as a means toward achieving just, harmonious communities that respect ecological constraints and the rights of children, women and handicapped, persons who are ill, and others. All major religions share these values, and that is why theologies of liberation, with their distinctive praxis concerns and social justice orientations, are appearing in all parts of the world. They do not have easy or magical answers, but they do have perspectives that are indispensable in our efforts to understand aspects of violence at their deepest level.

Institutionalized injustice and other forms of systemic violence do not remain external to persons. On the contrary, they often engender feelings of self-hatred, anger, frustration, violence and despair, which lead persons to individual acts of crime and violence. In this connection liberation theologians speak of a politics of conversion, to use Cornel West's phrase.[6] At the center of a politics of conversion are love, care and concern, as well as empowerment for ongoing struggle to transform persons as well as to reclaim neighborhoods and to create or transform cultural, political, economic and religious institutions so that the well-being of concrete persons and fulfillment of all their human needs are at the forefront of all agendas—religious and secular—to combat violence and to eradicate crime.

Reverend Paul Surlis is an associate professor of social ethics in the Department of Theology and Religious Studies at St. John's University in Jamica Queens. His areas of interest are Catholic social teaching, liberation theology and social ethics.

Notes:

1. Harvey, D. "Class Relations, Social Justice and the Politics of Difference," a public lecture in New York, August 8, 1992. I am indebted to this lecture for the class-focused analysis of this incident.

2. Gutièrrez, Gustavo, *A Theology of Liberation* (New York: Orbis Books, 1988).

3. Camara, Dom Helder, *Spiral of Violence* (Dimension Books, 1971).

4. National Conference of Catholic Bishops, *Economic Justice for All: Pastoral Letter on Catholic Social Teaching and the U.S. Economy* (Washington, D.C., 1986).

5. Brady, J. "The Social Economy of Arson: Vandals, Gangsters, Bankers, and Officials in the Making of an Urban Problem," in Greenberg, O.F. *Crime and Capitalism: Readings in Marxist Criminology* (Philadelphia: Temple University Press, 1993).

6. West, Cornel, *Race Matters* (Boston: Beacon Press, 1993), page 19.

Utilizing Just War Teaching to Condemn Modern War: A Reflection on the Developing Church Teaching*

By Rev. Francis X. Meehan

The main burden of this article will probably please neither those who strongly urge the church to repudiate, once and for all, its adherence to the just war teaching, nor those who are still convinced that a recourse to military force by a nation-state must remain a contemporary option for Christians. For in this article, while I will speak a word in defense of the just war teaching, it will be a paradoxical word. That is, I will attempt to show that the teaching's value lies in its very capacity to lead the whole church to a recognition of the injustice of all modern war.

One benefit of this approach is that it could give a fresh hope to those who are disappointed that the church has not repudiated its just war doctrine. A second benefit would be to suggest that the peace activist might seize a more fruitful line of advocacy. That is, rather than seek from the church a total repudiation of just war teaching, they might, instead, challenge the church to such a vigorous application of just war teaching as to preclude the possibility of justifying any modern war.

In fact, the key to all that I will say here is that it is precisely this vigorous application of the just war teaching, especially the criterion that forbids improportionate destruction, that is already leading the church through a process of a real doctrinal development in her teaching on war. This development also includes a new recognition of a deeper meaning of nonviolence in our time. I will attempt to unravel the main lines of this argument in four affirmations:

1) There are already clear signs of "development" going on within official and unoffical areas of church teaching, which come very close to condemning all modern war, even though, admittedly, that final step has not been taken.

2) Even though, in the theoretic order, nonviolence and just war teaching seem to be contradictories, in fact, in the concrete order just war teaching can lead the individual and the church to a posture of nonviolence, and this especially through a very rigorous application of the just war's one criterion requiring due proportion.

3) This movement of the church toward a posture of nonviolence need not and must not be accomplished in a sectarian manner. That is, there is a way for the church to adopt a posture of nonviolence without falling into an excessive withdrawal from the world. In fact, with the help of Gandhi's teaching, the Christian following of Jesus's Sermon can be seen as a secular wisdom which seeks not a private purity, but a public good.

4) A declericalized understanding of the Eucharistic call to holiness can foster an instinctual repugnance for modern war. Such a vision can lead to a new "sense of the faithful" that would actually accelerate a doctrinal development.

First Affirmation: There are already clear signs of development going on within official and unofficial areas of church teaching.

During the past three decades, many have challenged the church "to undertake an evaluation of war with an entirely new attitude." (*Constitution on the Church in the Modern World,* Art. 80). While the above phrase traces back to the Second Vatican Council, it also reflects the contemporary voices of many who even now challenge the church to a more prophetic critique of modern war — voices, that is, of theologians, peace organizations, individual bishops. One might ask, if the church were to develop her teaching into one that manifested "an entirely new attitude toward war," how would such a development take place? What would it look like?

A first place to start would be to recall the teaching of the Second Vatican Council itself. While it must be admitted that this Council's basic viewpoint remained within the structure of just war teaching, yet its very strong recognition of the way in which modern weaponry can inflict "indiscriminate havoc which goes far beyond the bounds of legitimate defense," can be taken as a sign that something is already happening within the modern church's theology of war. This insight of Vatican II into the dangers of modern weaponry, can be seen as an important milestone of a church that has already begun a journey of doctrinal development.

A second line of development concerns the church's view of nonviolence. That is, even if present church teaching continues to give a place of privilege to just war teaching, still, recent official documents have made a significant leap, not only in the respect they have accorded those who choose nonviolence, but also in their very understanding of the nature of nonviolence itself. Witness the statements of the United States bishops and, in fact, of all national hierarchies during the nuclear crisis of the early 1980s, as well as many statements of John Paul II in the past decade extolling nonviolence as an active intervention in the public order.

Notice, as an example, these very significant words of Pope John Paul II, as he reflected on the events in 1989:

> It seemed that the European order resulting from the Second World War could only be overturned by another war. Instead, it has been overcome by the nonviolent commitment of people who, while always refusing to yield to the force of power, suc-

ceeded time after time in finding effective ways of bearing witness to the truth." ("On the Hundredth Anniversary of Rerum Novarum   [Centesimus Annus]," 1991)

This success of nonviolent movements in Poland, Czechoslovakia, the Philippines and other countries is especially significant in that they allow many more people to grasp a richer understanding of nonviolence. That is, that nonviolence can no longer be restricted to a personal or private commitment, but clearly has a place for the pursuit of justice in the public order.

Over the recent years it is clear that within the thought of Pope John Paul II and other significant theological and Magisterial teaching sectors of the Catholic Church, a whole new reflection has begun to evolve. Theologian Drew Christiansen, on the occasion of the recent United Nations' intervention in Kosovo, outlined the manner in which John Paul II's teaching has evolved. It has moved from a stringent just war teaching toward a very strong affirmation of nonviolence. While this teaching has not been totally consistent, nor perfectly universal in its application, it has marked a significant development within official church reflection. (*America*, May 15, 1999)

Just as these teachings of John Paul II signify a new awareness within the teaching church, so similarly, in the Tenth Anniversary Statement of the United States Bishops (*The Harvest of Justice Is Sown in Peace*, November 17, 1993), nonviolence is seen not as an individualistic or passive option, but as an active force within the public order. In a significant paragraph titled "Nonviolence: New Importance," the Bishops say, "(The vision of nonviolence) ought not be confused with popular notions of nonresisting pacifism. For it consists of a commitment to resist manifest injustice and public evil with means other than force.... One must ask, in light of recent history, whether nonviolence should be restricted to personal commitments or whether it also should have a place in the public order with the tradition of justified and limited war." (*The Harvest of Justice*, Art. B-1)

Notice in the above statement a new recognition within church teaching not only of an experiential and concrete possibility of effective nonviolent activity, but also an explicit recognition that nonviolence's capacity for intervention in the public order could ultimately give it a whole new ethical status, as the church ponders its own response to a situation of conflict in the world. Such an understanding of nonviolence is already a long way from Vatican II's more minimalist call to merely respect the conscience of the individual pacifist.

Another sign that some definite movement within the church is already afoot can be seen in the deeper criticisms of war among what are usually regarded as very mainstream church sources. A perfect example of this occurred in July, 1991, when the prestigious Jesuit periodical *La Civiltà Cattolica* editorialized against the just war teaching, claiming that it was a teaching no longer relevant to the situation of modern war as we know it. (*La Civiltà Cattolica* [6 July 1991] English translation in *Origins* 21: 28 [19 December 1991] 450-54.) The article became somewhat of a *cause célèbre*, precisely because the periodical enjoys the reputation of frequently foreshadowing official church positions.

Some theologians felt that the article's theological claims against just war teaching fell short of the scientific rigor that one would hope to find in such a prestigious journal. Whether the critics of the article are correct or not, the point here is that the very existence of such an article published at this time signifies a new pastoral reality within the church, that is, a deeper uncomfortableness with war in general, and a growing resistance to accepting any particular modern war as just.

Critique of Just War Teaching Requires Honest Facing of Problems

This pastoral movement which more and more questions the justice of modern war is, I believe, something to be affirmed and celebrated. And along the journey of development, there is a ripening of reflection on all sides. At one point on the journey it may have been enough for the activist to stand back and challenge the church to adopt total nonviolence. But now the time has come when all of us, prophets and ordinary people, have to share the responsibility of trying to solve some of the honest problems that a total church posture of nonviolence can present — especially, in certain situations where defense against brutal oppression and deprivation of human rights seems to cry out for some use of force leveled against the aggressor. Allow me to say a brief word about this problem, even though I speak it more as a parenthesis to the main point of this article.

Today, in certain situations where grievous violations of human rights are taking place, or where chaos is inflicting great suffering on the weak, a call goes out, for example, for the U.N. or for the stronger nations to utilize military force. This use of military force has recently been termed "humanitarian intervention." Some will find the term a euphemism, but, regardless, the problem must be addressed. Recent interventions, such as occurred in Somalia, in Bosnia and in Kosovo provide an example which certainly challenges any total and puristic repudiation of just war teaching.

In these issues, given the difficulty of the question, it is no wonder then that the peace community itself has felt the sting of division. Moral theologian Kenneth Himes caught the issue succinctly when he wrote: "... that a group like Pax Christi would even debate the issue (of humanitarian military intervention) illustrates how human rights theory has complicated assessments of legitimate armed force. People who might be suspicious of war based on defense of state sovereignty now find themselves weighing the idea of military force for the sake of human rights." ("Just War, Pacifism and Humanitarian Intervention," *America*, Vol. 169 No. 4, August 14, 1993.)

While I certainly do not feel able within the confines of this article to adequately address such a terrible dilemma, I would like to make a more limited point. Namely, that when peace activists issue a moral call to the church asking her to finally declare the just war teaching as outmoded, and while that call may be prophetically powerful, nevertheless, they cannot and should not easily excuse themselves from the intellectual responsibility for elaborating how such a posture deals with all these very concrete factors in the moral equation, especially this central problem where basic justice and protection of the weak seems to require a form of coercion that is, at least, at the level of an international "police power."

However, all of this having been said, it still seems to this writer that it would be totally wrongheaded from both a spiritual and theological point of view to miss the crucial historical opportunity which the present questionings of the just war teaching present to the church. To dismiss out-of-hand a critical word, simply because a critic has not yet elaborated a totally coherent system, would be to risk missing the prophetic moment and method by which historical evolutions of moral doctrine can take place within the church.

And one way of not missing that moment is to try to imagine just exactly how a church, which for centuries has proclaimed a just war teaching, could ever embrace a seemingly contradictory development of condemning all modern war. Which point we now take up.

Second Affirmation: Even though, in the theoretic order, nonviolence and just war teaching seem to be contradictions, in fact, in the concrete order, just war teaching can lead the individual and the church to a posture of nonviolence, and this especially through a very rigorous application of the just war's one criterion requiring due proportion.

How can there be a mediating position between nonviolence, and just war teaching? One position clearly allows bloodshed, given all the right qualifications; the other position clearly forbids bloodshed. Is there a way out of the impasse? The bishops in their peace pastoral claimed that between nonviolence and just war teaching there is a "complementary relationship in the sense that both seek to serve the common good," and that "the two perspectives support and complement one another, each preserving the other from distortions." (*The Challenge of Peace*, Art. 121) Are the bishops speaking too irenically? How could the two ways be complementary?

I will suggest here that one way out of the impasse is to move from theory to the concrete. Sometimes ethical positions, seemingly diametrically opposed to one another, when put into the mix of concrete historical living, end up in remarkable convergence. Such a process may already be at work, and its outline may be as simple as this: First, people take a look at a given war as it is unfolding. They see its devastation, and clearly sense that it does not fulfill the criteria of the just war. They then begin to extend this vision to all modern war. Thus the condemnation of modern war can take place not through an ideological or theoretic repudiation of just war teaching, but through a concrete application of that teaching to the de facto destructiveness of all modern war.

In fact, this very utilization of just war categories to arrive at a condemnation of modern war seems to take place among peace activists, sometimes even unknowingly. That is, when one begins to analyze the rhetorical denunciations of the just war teaching, one often finds that the person has not really rejected the teaching itself, but rather the idea of an actual just war in today's circumstances. John Langan, in a review of the arguments between just war defenders and peace activists, catches this more concrete mode of arriving at nonviolence when he says, "Contemporary pacifism is not to be reduced to an abstract universal premise." (*Theological Studies*, March 1992)

And philosopher Jenny Teichman, in her work, *Pacifism and the Just War*, said this:

> Some believe that war is evil because violence is evil, some think that war is evil because killing human beings is evil, some believe that war is evil because large-scale killing of human beings is evil, some think war is evil because it necessarily involves the evil of killing innocent civilians. A principled person can become "anti-this" or "anti-that" not so much because of what "this" or "that" is in theory, but because of what "this" or "that" is, or must be, in practice.

Notice how her linking of different reasons for being against war helps us understand one meaning of the phrase, "complementary relationship." It is as simple as saying that, at the level of the concrete, the just war theorist can end up espousing the same option as the nonviolent person, that is, the option that is anti-war. That brings us to ask, what is it within the just war teaching which leads so many today to adopt a posture of total or at least almost total nonviolence?

The Proportionality Criterion of Just War Teaching

Probably the one single criterion of just war teaching, which can propel people to embrace nonviolence, is the "proportionality criterion." This criterion teaches "that the damage to be inflicted and the costs incurred by war must be proportionate to the good expected by taking up arms." (*The Challenge of Peace*, Art. 99)

The early Gulf War against Iraq is, in this writer's opinion, a perfect example of how improportionate destruction can begin to awaken people to a stand against all modern war. The process of reasoning is clear: One notices the widespread suffering and death of thousands of civilians and children in Iraq not only during the war, but after it as well. This recognition forces people to face up to how a war, even one supposedly based on surgical air strikes, violates just war teaching. (The Harvard team, which visited Iraq in April 1991, estimated that 170,000 children would die of gastrointestinal disease complicated by malnutrition as a result of the war.) This recognition of how one war can violate the criterion of due proportionality begins to extend then to all modern war.

It may not extend to every form of forceful police action as a defense against tyranny. At the very time of submission of this article we are dealing with the aftermath of the U.N. intervention in Kosovo. There were those who argued for a legitimate police action in Kosovo preventing further brutalities against Ethnic Albanians. But some of the same defenders of such an international intervention also criticized the United Nations tactic of bombing Belgrade. This they felt moved from police action to actual war and began to clearly violate, not only due proportion, but also the principle of civilian immunity.

However, there is within recent church teaching, that it is more and more willing to repudiate all war-like actions, not just during or after a post-war analysis of various violations, but as an insight of the dynamism of war itself. As regards the papal teaching on this issue of proportionality, Bryan Hehir, the influential theologian for the Bishops Conference, suggests that the key argument of Pope John Paul II in his January 1991 letter to President Bush rested on "fears of disproportionate results." (*The Tablet,* June 1991) In other words, Pope John Paul II utilized the proportionality criterion, not as a post-factum argument about how the war was being conducted, but as a questioning of the very right to enter the war. (In the technical language of just war teaching, he was using the proportionality criterion not only as an "in bello" argument against war (i.e. illicit conduct within a war) but as an "ad bellum argument" (i.e. an argument against the very right to prosecute this particular war).

This judgment about the proportionality of modern war is based precisely on how modern weaponry really functions today. That is, the weaponry of our day possesses an inbuilt intentionality to destroy what was precisely destroyed in Iraq, namely the civilian infrastructure of the country. Such a judgment need not wait till after the fact. For is it not exactly this infrastructure that the weaponry of modern war guarantees to be destroyed? Thus it is that this issue of proportionality, in the concrete world in which we live, tilts us not only toward a negative judgment toward a particular war, but can be the key factor in tilting many against all modern war.

In this respect the writings of Pope John Paul II, according to Father Hehir in the article mentioned above, have manifested an evolution, which, while they may not have reached an absolute condemnation of all war, nevertheless contain an increasing pessimism toward the human capacity to contain modern warfare within reasonable limits.

And it is precisely this inbuilt guarantee of war's breaking the bounds of proportionality that poses a key challenge for the church today. How can the church fulfill her moral and prophetic role unless she does, in fact, use the proportionality criterion not merely as a judgment as to how a war is being fought (an "in bello" criterion), but as an ante-factum denunciation of war? In fact, one could suggest from experience that, once a war has started, it seems that any church witness or judgment about proportionality becomes very ineffective.

It is these two simple facts, namely, the inevitable use of weaponry that has an inbuilt intentionality of improportionate destruction, and the challenge to the church to give more effective witness against such destructiveness, that lead many, including this writer, to continue to defend the value of the just war teaching, and at the same time to urge the church to adopt a total posture of condemnation of all modern war.

Such a development within the church is not characterized by saying that the church is "repudiating just war teaching." Rather, it is more that the church from the experience of her people comes to the conviction that in the concrete world there is only one way to fulfill just war teaching, namely through a presumption that no war today can truly fulfill the requirements of just war teaching, or in other words that today there can be no truly just war.

Such a presumption, if it were to be arrived at officially and authoritatively, would be principled, even though it is arrived at inductively, concretely and experientially. Such a way of arriving at an ethical truth may not be distant from the way all Christian ethical truths may have had their origin. Perhaps that is how even Jesus came to speak such a strong teaching against violence, but more on that later. For now let us address one important theological problem that is often presented as an obstacle to the church's adopting such a total condemnation of modern war.

Third Affirmation: This movement of the church toward a posture of nonviolence need not and must not be accomplished in a sectarian manner. That is, there is a way for the church to adopt a posture of nonviolence without falling into an excessive withdrawal from the world. In fact, with the help of Gandhi's teaching, the Christian following of Jesus's Sermon can be seen as a secular wisdom which seeks not a private purity, but a public good.

The theological problem can be phrased in the form of a question: How could there be a total church movement toward nonviolence without the church finding itself in a sect-like posture of withdrawal from the world, thereby diminishing its critical interaction with public policy? This is a very real and legitimate concern that theologians present against any suggested church evolution toward a total posture of nonviolence. They fear that such a movement would constitute a "sectarian turn," that is, a withdrawal from the world that would be excessive and would also go against a strong tradition of church respect for world structures, and a healthy sharing of human responsibility in a world of ambiguity.

This is of course a difficult theological issue. The accusation of sectarianism in theological circles often becomes a real conversation-stopper. Who wants to be sectarian? The question itself brings up that key ecclesiological issue which confronted the Second Vatican Council, especially the writers of *The Pastoral Constitution.* How can the church radically criticize certain basic social structures of the world and still remain in responsible dialogue? This very question forces us to reflect more carefully about the very meaning of nonviolence today, and how a turn toward nonviolence by the church is to be accomplished. Allow me to make two points which I hope will be helpful.

The first point I wish to make is that, from our place in history, now almost 50 years after the death of Mahatma Gandhi, we must recognize that nonviolence has taken on a new and public face. We have already alluded in our first section above to statements of John Paul II and the U.S. Bishops which have caught this public face of nonviolence. But let us develop it more clearly now.

John Dunne in his recent work, *Peace of the Present: An Un-violent Way of Life*, makes clear that Gandhi even in his time was forced to address the sectarian issue. His critics accused him of saying that the nonviolent way was really the pursuit of "personal holiness at the expense of the public good." But Gandhi never gave up insisting that it was both.

If we look at nonviolence through this Gandhian prism, that is, as a way of seeking the common good, if we see nonviolence as a strategy for pursuing justice, then it is no longer simply a protection of one's religious purity. In other words, nonviolence need not be chosen from an "ethic of obedience," but from one of Christian responsibility for the world. From this perspective the option for nonviolence has moved beyond an act of sectarian fidelity.

Secondly, if the Gandhian revolution allows us to look at nonviolence in a fresh manner, are we not also to grasp a similarly fresh understanding of the words of Jesus himself? That is, Gandhi's revolution invites us to think of Jesus' Sermon on the Mount in a new way. Let us unfold this very briefly here: Jesus says, "You have heard the commandment, 'an eye for an eye, a tooth for tooth.' But what I say to you is: offer no resistance to injury. When a person strikes you on the right cheek, turn and offer the other." (Mt 5:38-39) After Gandhi, can we not understand this injunction of Jesus, as more than a personal religious calling (sectarian)? Is it not moreso a wisdom grounded in universal human experience?

In this regard I received fresh insight from a recent philosophical study on nonviolence by Donald Scherer and James Child titled *Two Paths Toward Peace* (Temple University Press, 1992). Scherer helps us understand even the secular wisdom of Jesus' teaching by an unlikely finding. He alludes to an ethos of certain West African tribes, and explains how their rules on handling aggression provide for the re-establishing of a structure of social intercourse rather than focusing on who was wrong. In this way the tribes, in handling the mediation between an aggressor and a victim, look at more than just who is right or wrong, but at a commonality between aggressor and victim that allows for a long range possibility of healing the whole tribe.

Such an insight can suddenly put the words of Jesus in a new light. Take the great text concerning love of enemies. Jesus says: "My command to you is: love your enemies, pray for your persecutors. This will prove that you are children of your heavenly Creator, for the sun rises on the bad and the good, God rains on the just and the unjust." (Mt 5: 44-45) In this text we can sense precisely what Scherer pointed out, namely how Jesus catches the perspective of commonality between aggressor and the aggrieved.

The implication here is to say that, what Gandhi saw, Jesus also saw, namely, that violence is causative of later violence, that it brings about a social after-effect that contributes to the eruption of later violence. It is this cyclic and "mimetic" characteristic of war which is so much neglected by just war teaching. (For the meaning of violence's mimetic character, that is, its capacity to incite imitation, see, Rene Girard, *Things Hidden Since the Foundation of the World,* Stanford, California, 1987.) Witness, for example the long delayed effects of violence in the ethnic and nationalistic eruptions that are occurring now after the break-up of the Soviet Empire.

The vision of Gandhi and this insight of Jesus into the common humanity of the aggressor and the aggrieved help us to understand the broad historical perspective of nonviolence. And it is this perspective which gives a vision that is the very antithesis of sectarianism. That is, a Catholic who followed Jesus' ethic would be doing so, not merely as a mode of religious purity, but because the wisdom of Jesus is a wisdom that would help the Christian speak to the long-range secular concerns of justice and peace in a given community of peoples. In other words it is not as though nonviolence simply disregards the issue of justice or the issue of aggrieved rights. Rather, by seeking to find a creative way out of conflict, it attempts to guard a long-range justice, one that will perdure. Thus it is unfair to dichotomize work for justice over and against a nonviolent nurturing of peace. Today, we know that there can be a nonviolent form of action that also works for justice.

In an age when we have seen nonviolence play a part in revolutionary events in the Philippines, in Poland, in Czechoslovakia, in Russia, in South Africa, in Latin America, even in China, it would be tragic and most ironic, if we in the church were to miss how a posture of nonviolence could still maintain a healthy dialogue with worldly concerns of justice.

However, if there is ever to be a real development of doctrine, these insights into nonviolence, and the repugnance to the improportionate destructiveness of war must impact a wider circle of people in the church. It cannot be only a moral or intellectual elite, who seek, as it were, "to enlighten" all the others. Rather a whole new imagination is needed. At one level this imagination will be a concrete imaging of what modern war is really all about. But at another level there is a directly spiritual imagination needed, about who the Christian is, and what the Christian stands for in this world. As an example of this latter point, I would like to broach a brief reflection on how simple insight into the lay person's role at the Eucharist can provoke a new imagination within the church itself.

Fourth Affirmation: A declericalized vision of the Christian call to holiness could foster an instinctual repugnance for seeing modern war as compatible with the Christian celebration of Eucharist.

When it comes to the question of war, arguments can tend to remain very abstract. That is, people tend to argue about war in general, but they do not often imagine what it would be like, if they themselves had to engage in the fighting. One of the great seminal theologians of our time, Father Bernard Lonergan always insisted that we can never neglect the subtle relationship between ethical theory and our own personal involvement. (*Method in Theology*, 237-244) It seems to this writer that if religious people would relate ethical theorizing on the legitimacy of war to questions of their own personal involvement in a particular war, we might see an even more pronounced evolution of ethical thinking within the church.

Just as an example, an idea occurred to me during my own questioning regarding the recent Gulf War. At that time I had to ask myself, if I were to defend the justice of this war, would I be willing to drop the bombs or fire the weaponry myself? In reflecting on this, I remembered how Thomas Aquinas in his *Summa Theologica* dealt with the prohibition of a priest's involvement in bloodshed. Aquinas based his prohibition on the cleric's involvement with the Eucharist:

> Now warlike pursuits are altogether incompatible with the duties of a cleric...because the clerical Orders are directed to the ministry of the altar, on which the Passion of Christ is represented sacramentally... (IIa IIae 40 2.)

Suddenly it came to me, that if Thomas Aquinas could have an aversion to allowing the hands that touched the Eucharist also to inflict bloodshed, then it is a short step to recognizing that lay people today also touch the Eucharist, and to carry forward the implications of that for a development of doctrine in the church. I am appealing here, not to a mere piety, nor to a nostalgic clerical mystique about the hands that touched the Eucharist. Rather, I am suggesting that there is within the church a new recognition of how all the people, not merely the priest, are really called to "touch the Eucharist," and how through this they are to become a prophetic leaven in the world. In other words I am taking Thomas Aquinas's 13th century instinct regarding the role of the priest, and extending it to what could be a 21st century "instinct of the faithful" regarding the relationship of Eucharist to modern war. For Thomas the priests' hands that touched the Eucharist should not be used to shed blood. So today all the people are called to the holiness that becomes a prophetic sign of the peace brought about by the sacrament of Jesus' death.

It strikes me that this simple recognition, especially when brought to concrete imagination, that is, when it really engages, not only an abstract question of war, but a concrete question about my own involvement in the dropping of bombs... then this recognition may go a long way toward a development of doctrine regarding the legitimacy of a Christian's participation in modern war. This line of reasoning need not bypass just war categories. Rather, the just war principles will be strengthened by an instinct that senses the incompatibility of, on the one hand, receiving Eucharist, and on the other hand involving oneself in the form of destruction which modern war implies.

Concluding Summary

It should be clear by now, that the burden of this paper is to suggest that there is another prophetic path, one that does not repudiate just war teaching, but simply calls the church to more vigorously apply it, so that she will reach a position that sees all modern war as unjust. This church dissent from war will follow the Sermon of Jesus of Matthew 5, but not in a sectarian manner. Rather Jesus' words will be seen as a gift of wisdom to help communities and nations avoid the violence that inevitably becomes improportionate.

Thus the Christian will not carve out for himself or herself a private peace, but by reading Jesus through a Gandhian prism, will find creative and active forms of nonviolence that truly seek justice in the public order. Such a movement within the church will be enhanced and will become more accessible to a wider number of people through a new imagination of what it means for all Christians to celebrate Eucharist. And through all of this there can take place within the church a development of doctrine which truly does respond to the Second Vatican Council's call "to undertake an evaluation of war with an entirely new attitude."

Francis X. Meehan is the pastor of SS Simon and Jude Parish in West Chester, Pa., the author of A Contemporary Social Spirituality *(Orbis Press), along with many articles, and a member of Pax Christi USA.*

*This is a substantial revision and updating of an article which appeared in a book, *Studying War-No More?* (Kok Pharos Kampen: The Netherlands, 1993) published under the auspices of Pax Christi International and edited by Brian Wicker. Sections and thoughts from this earlier article are used here with full permission of Pax Christi International.

Notes

1. Recently I took up this point in a column, "On Carefully Critiquing the *Just War* Teaching," the *Pax Christi Magazine*, 16:4 (Winter 1991) 15.

2. Heinz Schuster defines the task of today's pastoral theology: "To examine the contemporary situation and find in it a summons of God to the church reminding it of its ever new task of formulating and announcing the gospel of Jesus...." "Pastoral Theology," in Karl Rahner (ed.), *Encyclopedia of Theology: The Concise Sacramentum Mundi*, (New York: Seabury Press, 1975) p.1180.

3. The Second Vatican Council, even though it praised pacifism, nevertheless clearly came down on the side of just-war teaching. See *The Pastoral Constitution of the Church in the Modern World*, Art. 79. For

a sidelight on one peace advocate's experience in this discussion, see James W. Douglass, *The Nonviolent Coming of God* (Maryknoll, New York: Orbis Books), 98-103.

4. *The Challenge of Peace: God's Promise and Our Response*, Art. 120

5. *La Civiltà Cattolica* (6 July 1991). English Translation in *Origins* 21:28 (19 December 1991) 450-54.

6. John P. Langan, S.J., "The Just War Theory After the Gulf War," *Theological Studies* 53:1 (March 1992) 100-103.

7. *The Challenge of Peace*, Art.120-21.

8. In a quote I cannot now locate, Thomas Merton once claimed with some irony that, while theoretically there was room for the just war doctrine, in practice, given the conditions of modern war, he found it necessary to be a pacifist.

9. Karl Rahner, S.J., *The Christian of the Future* (New York: Herder and Herder, 1967), pp. 39-48.

10. In an earlier column I attempted to outline how this process might take place. See Francis X. Meehan, "Nonviolence and the Bishops' Pastoral Letter, A Case for a Development of Doctrine," *Thought* 59:232 (March 1984) 25-40. The article may also be found in Judith Dwyer, ed., *The Catholic Bishops and Nuclear War* (Washington D.C., Georgetown University Press), 1984.

11. Langan, 100

12. Jenny Teichman, *Pacifism and the Just War* (New York: Basil Blackwell Inc., 1986), 107-108.

17. John Langan in the article mentioned above says, "The Gulf War

case shows that we need to think about extending the list of inappropriate targets to those systems that are necessary for the survival of the civilian population." 110. I agree with this statement except that to me "think about" does not seem strong enough. Is it not clear that such inappropriate targets are already forbidden by the just war teaching?

19. Albert Camus touches on this problem of ambiguity in a 1948 speech to a group of Dominicans: In a choice between the forces of terror and the forces of dialogue, he fears Christianity might not be up to the task: "It may be... that Christianity will insist... on giving its condemnations the obscured form of the encyclical." *Resistance Rebellion and Death* (The Modern Library, Knopf, 1960), 55-56.

20. I developed these reasons in slightly more detail in a column, "For Pastoral Leaders: Transforming Just-War Teaching," *Pax Christi USA Magazine*, 16:1 (spring, 1991) 25.

21. Langan, 102-112.

22. See Charles Moeller, "History of the Pastoral Constitution," in H. Vorgrimler, *Commentary on the Documents of Vatican II*, Vol 5 (New York: Herder and Herder, 1969), especially 8-10.

23. Kenneth Himes suggests that people "talk past one another" in using these terms "church and sect." See "Nuclear Pacifism in the U.S.: Responding as Church or Sect," in a report by Lisa Sowle Cahill, "Seminar on Moral Theology," Proceedings of the Forty-First Annual Convention, Catholic Theological Society of America, 154-55.

24. Both Pope John XXIII and Cardinal Suenens used the terms ad intra and ad extra to describe the effort of the Council and specifically *The Pastoral Constitution.* See Charles Moeller, "History...," 8.

25. Quoted in B.R. Nanda, *Gandhi and His Critics* (Delhi: Oxford

University Press, 1985), p.4 as cited in John Dunne, *Peace of the Present: An Un-violent Way of Life* (Notre Dame, Indiana; University of Notre Dame Press), 34.

26. Gandhi's words: "It (nonviolence) is to begin with oneself, eliminating all the hatred from one's heart, but not to stop with oneself." As cited in Dunne, ibid, 37. Thomas Merton distills citations from Gandhi's political vision in his *Gandhi on Non-Violence* (New York: New Directions Press, 1965), 51-62.

27. Nonviolence today has developed an autonomous existence beyond religious moorings. Gene Sharp's three-volume work would be an example of non-religious writing. Gene Sharp, *The Politics of Nonviolent Action* (Boston: Porter Sargent, 1973).

28. The phrase, "a completely fresh reappraisal" is taken from *The Pastoral Constitution*, Art. 80.

29. Robert Ellsberg provides a handy glossary of Gandhi's terms in his recently edited work, *Gandhi on Christianity* (Maryknoll, New York: Orbis Books), xviii. Ahimsa is usually translated as nonviolent love; satyagraha signifies a "truth-force" or nonviolent resistance.

30. 1 Corinthians 1:23.

31. Matthew 5:38-39.

32. Donald Scherer and James Child, *Two Paths Toward Peace* (Philadelphia: Temple University Press, 1992).

33. Ibid. 36-44.

34. Scherer appeals to what he calls Gandhi's teleology: "...any resort to violence, though it may appear to do good, does only temporary good, while the evil in the violence causes later harm." Gandhi

believed that "violence always creates a social malaise that contributes to the eruption of later violence." Ibid. 44-45 He suggests that just-war theorists tend to ignore this broad social malaise when they attempt to examine the "greater good" or proportionality. In effect he is saying that the just war teaching vision is historically too narrow.

35. Matthew 5:44-45.

36. Philosopher Rene Girard captures this causality of violence by his use of the word "mimetic." Violence is mimed, imitated. (Rene Girard, *Things Hidden Since the Foundation of the World*, Trans. Stephen Bann and Michael Metteer (Stanford, California: Stanford U. Press, 1987), p. 137 as cited in Dunne, ibid. p. 40. John Dunne succinctly calls it the Hatfield-McCoy syndrome. 22.

37. Bernard Haring asks: "Have we, moral theologians and church leaders, fulfilled our role of healing and revealing in this decisive field?" *The Healing Power of Peace and Nonviolence* (Mahwah, N.J: Paulist Press, 1986), 3.

38. See Bernard Lonergan, S.J., *Method in Theology*, New York: Herder and Herder, 1972), 104-104; 161-162; 237-244. See also John Haughey, S.J., where he speculates about limitations of the just-war teaching in calling us to a moral about-face. "Disarmament of the Heart," in Philip J. Murnion ed., *Catholics and Nuclear War: A Commentary on the Challenge of Peace* (New York: Crossroad, 1983), p. 225.

THE THEOLOGY OF PEACEMAKING

By Mary Elsbernd, OSF

It is a crisp night with huge, floppy snowflakes ambling their way into soft sculptured mounds in the yard outside. But I am inside, in my favorite chair, fascinated again by the lights on the Christmas tree. After the joyful noises of the day's events, I relish the silence pregnant with peace in the closing moments of Christmas day. My mind wanders through the "peace of Christmas," that stranger's smile, warm greetings from the neighbors we hardly ever see, the songs everyone knows, a self-made gift from a dear friend. Even the newspapers are filled with stories of peace on earth and good will to those usually forgotten. The fleeting nature of such happenings brings out cynicism in some, but not in me. I am awed yearly that the celebration of Jesus' birth nearly 2000 years after its occurrence can still bring peace to this old earth—even if it is only for a few days in the darkest, coldest season of the year. Yet I maintain that the reason peace returns each year at Christmas rests more in who Jesus is than in Jesus' words about peace. I find in that peace the hope and the promise that, throughout the year, Christians can be the peace that is Jesus.

* * *

1. Jesus: The Incarnate God

Christmas celebrates a central tenet of the Christian tradition. Jesus is the fullness of divinity and the fullness of humanity. Neither the humanity nor the divinity of Jesus negates the other. Throughout the ages, people have grappled with this wondrous mystery and probed its significance for Christian living. The evangelists Matthew and Luke find it significant to include the human ancestry of Jesus in their infancy narratives (Matthew 1:1-17; Luke 3:23-28), although they both testify that the conception of Jesus was the work of the Holy Spirit (Matthew 1:18-20; Luke 1:35). According to these authors, both

Joseph (Matthew 1:19-24) and Mary (Luke 1:26-37) sought to understand what this child meant.

Throughout the ages, the Christian faithful have continued to wrestle with the fact of an incarnate God in Jesus. Although the divinity of Jesus (Docetism) or the humanity of Jesus (Arianism) was at times overemphasized, Christians continued to affirm that Jesus was fully human and fully divine.

"The Pastoral Constitution on the Church in the Modern World" gives words to this phenomenon:

> He [Jesus] who is "the image of the invisible God" (Colossians 1:15), is Himself the perfect man (sic)....Since human nature as He assumed it was not annulled, by that very fact it has been raised up to a divine dignity in our respect too. For by His incarnation the Son of God has united Himself in some fashion with every man (sic). He worked with human hands, He thought with a human mind, acted by human choice, and loved with a human heart.[1]

This paragraph begins to suggest some of the implications of an incarnate God for daily Christ living. Because Jesus is fully human and fully divine, the transcendent dimension of earthly reality is affirmed.

Human persons today are carriers of the divine. The divine Spirit of Jesus dwells in human hearts (John 14:23-26) urging that the incarnation of God in this world be completed (John 14:10,12). From John's perspective, the works of Jesus are the faithful embodiment of God's loving presence among the people. The disciple is called to continue these works of Jesus. The story is told of soldiers passing through Italy at the end of World War II. In a village, they came upon a statue of the Christ that the wartime ravages had left without hands or feet. One of the soldiers made a sign reminding the passersby, "Today Christ has no hands or feet but yours." Such an attitude testifies that the incarnation was not only a past event involving one person, Jesus, in whom God was radically embodied. Rather, the Christian community continues to be the body of Christ; the divine dwells in and among the people of God. Inasmuch as the transcendent God is present in the Christian community, the incarnation of God persists.

The incarnation proclaims not only that human persons are bearers of the divine, but also that the whole world shares in that potential. The biological food chain is a somewhat elemental witness to that fact. In the letter to the Romans, Paul recalls the potential of creation to "share in the glorious freedom of the children of God" (Romans 8:20-22). In a similar recognition of creation's potential to show forth the divine, Gerard Manley Hopkins writes:

> The world is charged with the grandeur of God.
> It will flame out, like shining from shook foil;
> It gathers to a greatness, like the ooze of oil
> Crushed. Why do men (sic) then now not reck his rod?
> Generations have trod, have trod, have trod;
> And all is seared with trade; bleared, smeared with toil;
> And wears man's (sic) smudge and shares man's (sic) smell: the soil
> Is bare now, nor can foot feel, being shod.
> And for all this, nature is never spent;
> There lives the dearest freshness deep down things;
> And though the last lights off the black West went
> Oh, morning, at the brown brink eastward, springs—
> Because the Holy Ghost over the bent
> World broods with warm breast and with ah! bright wings.[2]

Hopkins is quick to point out, however, that this potential is not always recognized. Generations have trod upon the obvious reflection of the divine. It is seared, bleared, smeared and smudged, until it smells of human effort. In fact, humanity has shod itself against the bare, divine grandeur. Creation can be exploited as well as reverenced. The human transformation of the world can be death-dealing as well as life-giving. Human efforts in the universe can embody immediate egotism as well as the transcendent God. Jesus the incarnate God endures as the persistent claim that the whole of created reality is theophany, the "stuff" that mediates the transcendent God. Or, in Hopkins' words, still "the Holy Ghost over the bent world broods with warm breast and with ah! bright wings."

The person of Jesus, described by the Christian tradition as fully human and fully divine, seems to call into question a life approach that clearly highlights opposites. It is so easy to augment what separates black from white, female from male, young from old, East from West, that the lifestance itself can degenerate into a field of "us" versus "them" maneuvers. "They" are inferior; "they" are threatening "our" way of life and should be avoided; "they" cannot be trusted. Jesus was not either divine or human, but rather lived the Christological tension of human and divine. It would seem that the disciples of Jesus, too, must seek to embody that same tension of seeming opposites.

This could mean that a disciple gives at least as much reign to the divine dimension of Christian living as to the human. It could also mean some attitudinal adjustment toward those others who don't share the same world view or lifestyle as the disciple. Or this could mean the active promotion of unity in parishes, neighborhoods and peace groups, despite differences and difficulties.

Not long ago, the Diocesan Council of Catholic Women and the Association of Women Religious of Sioux City, Iowa, joined in hostessing an evening of reflection, Women Gathered for Peace. One of the striking features of the evening was the diversity of opinions articulated and listened to around one common table—without raised

49

voices or clenched fists. Women belonging to Beyond War talked with women belonging to the Blue Army. Quaker women brought their long pacifist tradition to the table with women who could call this their first exposure to peace thinking. But there they were, women talking together around tables in spite of diverse views and different opinions.

The tension of opposing viewpoints seeking common ground and common action appears to be more in keeping with the mystery of Jesus the incarnate God than groups promoting programs that exclude those of other persuasions.

2. Jesus: The Reconciliation of God

The incarnate one, Jesus, is the reconciliation of God. Jesus is the one who overcomes the historically accrued divisiveness between God and human persons, between human groups, as well as between human persons and the created world. In Jesus, the human choices against the created peace in the beginning are overturned. In Jesus, God is reconciling humanity, indeed the whole world, into the harmony of the beginning.

The New Testament presents a recurrent cluster of ideas in its descriptions of reconciliation. The reconciliation that means peace is God's action through Jesus Christ (Romans 5:1; Ephesians 2:13; Colossians 1:20) in an earthy, fleshy body (Romans 5:9; Ephesians 2:15; Colossians 1:20). In Jesus, God promises faithful love to those who reject God's mercy. In the television miniseries, "Jesus of Nazareth" by Franco Zeffirelli, Jesus announces God's reconciling action: "The distance between you and God is vast. No human steps can cross it. Here is the good news: You don't have to cross it. God is coming to save you, even the most wretched. Do not shut the door in the face of God."

In this announcement, Jesus proclaimed the absence of God's wrath toward sinful humanity and announced a new reality: Human life is not about appeasing a vengeful God, but about responding to God's saving love in Jesus. Although the whole of Jesus' ministry proclaimed this new reality, it was particularly concentrated in the death of Jesus on the cross (Romans 5:8; Ephesians 2:13-14; Colossians 1:21). Jesus entered the human condition, including death.

As an incarnation of the holy, Jesus embodied not only God's love for all peoples, but also the depth of human love's response for God. Jesus did not shut a door in the face of God. Instead, Jesus modeled a life without hostility toward God or others. In Jesus, the disciples witnessed the possibility of a personal relationship with the God whose love had crossed over the gulf made by sin. The whole life and death of Jesus showed how human persons through faith can live reconciled with God. Jesus accomplished reconciliation because Jesus is reconciliation.

Prior to Jesus, enmity reigned: enmity between the peoples and God (Romans 5:10; Ephesians 2:12-13; Colossians 1:21), between the major divisions of peoples at that time (Galatians 3:28), and within all of the natural world (Colossians 1:20). The death of Jesus brought peace with God (Romans 5:1) and access in the Spirit to God (Ephesians 2:18; Colossians 1:22). For Paul, the wonder of Jesus' reconciling activity was that Jesus died for sinners, thus proving God's immense love for all those whose human choices had separated themselves from that love (Romans 5:6-8). Since Jesus' death, no longer were people enemies of God, for God in Jesus had come to dwell in their midst and in their hearts through the Spirit of Jesus.

The Torah, the Jewish law, had insisted that the Jews live in separation from the Gentiles who did not know the covenant. Through death on the cross for all, Jesus broke down this enmity that kept Jew and Gentile apart. It was not, however, by making Jews into Gentiles or Gentiles into Jews. Rather, in Jesus there is one new creation, neither Jew nor Gentile. In Jesus, one new person was created from those who had been two (Ephesians 2:15-16). This meant peace between those who had been enemies. Such an understanding is consistent with Paul's presentation of justification by faith apart from the Jewish law or Gentile wisdom. Jesus, however, was not only the reconciliation between Gentile and Jew, but also between male and female, as well as slave and free. Through faith in Jesus, symbolized by Christian baptism into Jesus, all Christians are one in Jesus (Galatians 3:27-29; 1 Corinthians 12:13; Colossians 3:11).

The letter to the Colossians expands the reconciliation effected through Jesus' death on the cross, extending that reconciliation to all things on earth and in heaven (Colossians 1:20). Again, this application is consistent with the portrayal of the cosmic Christ in the letter as a whole. The reconciliation through Jesus' death makes peace with God (Romans 5:1; Colossians 1:22), with Jew and Gentile (Ephesians 2:15), and with everything (Colossians 1:20).

The final recurring element in this concept of Jesus as the reconciliation of God offers an understanding of Christian life. The new Christian community is reminded that, although they are already reconciled in Christ, they must strive to be reconciled (Romans 5:9; Ephesians 2:22; Colossians 1:23). In keeping with the incarnational nature of Christianity, this unity in Jesus needs to be enacted within the community. Two recurring characteristics of such a Christian community appear to be a peaceable life together and love of those who call Christians enemy (Matthew 5:38-45; Romans 12:9-21). There is no place for disunity among people made one in the Jesus who overcame these divisions. The apostle Paul continues. Not only has God in Jesus overturned the enmity of the people toward God, toward each other and the whole world, but God also made those in Christ ministers of reconciliation (2 Corinthians 5:19-20). All those who are the body of Jesus Christ continue to be agents of God's reconciling activity in the world. Reconciliation in Christ Jesus is not a one-time accomplishment, but an ongoing process, which Christians complete by their living.

It is against this background of Jesus as the reconciliation of God that one can interpret the words of Jesus. After the beatitudes, the Sermon on the Mount speaks of six antithetical statements: "You have heard that it was said...But I say to you..." (Matthew 5:21,22ff). With these comments, the authoritative understanding of Jesus is contrasted with the popular interpretation of the law. What the law had established as restrictions on disproportionate vengeance, Jesus radicalizes as the demands of interior conversion to the message of reconciliation. Two of the antitheses are of particular interest, since they specifically address reconciliation and response to coercion.

In the section on murder, Matthew 5:23-24 presents the situation of a worshipper who recalls that someone is holding a grudge against her. Jesus urges her to leave her cultic activities and to seek reconciliation, even though she apparently is not at fault. The reader is left with the sense of the urgency of reconciliation with one's neighbor: It takes precedence over cultic ritual, and it requires initiative, even when one is innocent of disharmony. The same urgent injunction is repeated in verses 25-26 with an example of legal action.

The second antithesis touches on the subject of retaliation. Jesus not only requires an end to retaliatory activity in the face of physical violence (Matthew 5:39), legal cases (5:40), forced military conscription (5:41), and personal imposition (5:42), but also obliges active non-resistance to such infringement on self- interest. Neither retaliation nor resistance is an appropriate response to those who have been reconciled to God in Jesus.[3]

Instead, the message of Jesus promotes a response that makes a positive contribution to the demise of the cycle of violent actions and counteractions. The disciple of reconciliation is to initiate reconciliation regardless of who is at fault in the breach of relationship. The follower of Jesus responds to imposition by originating more than what was demanded.

Jesus as the reconciliation of God confronts the Christian community with a number of dimensions. Reconciliation claims both human and divine roles in peace. Although reconciliation is the work of God in Jesus, it is in the human body and death of Jesus that reconciliation is effected. In addition, reconciliation is the creation of something new (2 Corinthians 5:17; Ephesians 2:15), the creation of one new entity from those who had been two. Thus, the enmity between God and humanity is overcome in Jesus. Jew and Greek, male and female are in Christ one new creation. Lastly, reconciliation is not a static accomplished fact, but an objective beginning, which awaits completion in and through the ongoing human ministry of reconciliation.

3. The Risen Jesus

God's reconciling activity in Jesus was most evident in the death-reconciliation event. Through the resurrection of Jesus, God gave the divine response to human suffering as well as to injustice and violence.

Jesus entered into suffering and death believing in the God whose life he embodied and whose faithful love he revealed. God's response to the human attempts to terminate divine life and love made incarnate was the fullness of a new way of living: resurrection. The resurrection of Jesus is God's response not only to this one specific instance of suffering and death, but also to centuries of death-dealing activities in wars, collective human misery and solitary personal pain. The Risen Jesus stands as a testimony that the God of Jesus is definitively for life, for unexpected life even through pain and death.

The God of Jesus presents the believer with the possibility of choosing to embody that which is life-giving, even when the personal or institutional forces of the environment are death-dealing.

The resurrection victory over death invites the disciples of the Risen Jesus to encourage the development of gifts and talents, rather than to withhold confirmation. The resurrection urges the support of others in their life ventures, instead of institutional individualism. Jesus' victory over death dares disciples to love one another faithfully, in lieu of apathetic non-response. The resurrection encourages a joy of living, in place of a stern shouldering up of obligation. Jesus' victory over death promotes career choices that serve life among the human community, instead of individual gain or social erosion. The resurrection presents the Christian today with a reason to believe that life-giving decisions remain real options, in spite of cumulative choices to the contrary.

Life-giving options would be more attractive if they did not entail personal cost or dying. But the Risen Jesus recalls that the life that is God's gift comes through suffering and death, not in spite of such pain. The Risen Jesus not only proclaims that life has overcome death, but also how death has been overcome, namely through the path of suffering (*Church in the Modern World*, 22; Matthew 16:24-26; Romans 8:17-25). A life that encourages others' talents could mean setting aside efficiency, or even one's own expertise, so others can become skilled. A life supportive of others may mean going against certain institutionalized ways of treating others. Faithful love gives a priority to what is best for the beloved, even when it is not personally convenient. Careers oriented to service of the human community rarely result in wealth or status. Living in the hope of the resurrection comes no easier for the Christian disciple today than it did for Jesus at the agony in the garden.

The resurrection is not only about life's victory over death. It is also about the divine response to violence and injustice. Violence and injustice were the fabric of the trial and crucifixion of Jesus. The resurrection proclaims the limited jurisdiction of violence and injustice. The response of God to the unjust violence unleashed on Jesus was neither anger nor revenge. Rather, the Spirit of Jesus was handed over to the disciples that they might continue the ministry of reconciliation. The Spirit—the gift of peace—and the ministry of Jesus: such was the divine response to violence and injustice.

In the Gospel of John, the death of Jesus is reported with a singular expression: Jesus "handed over the spirit" (John 19:30). Scholars hold that John intentionally used this atypical expression for dying to point out that the Spirit was passed on to the Christian community through the death of Jesus. Jesus had promised the Spirit to the disciples (Luke 24:49; John 14:26), and after the resurrection, the Spirit came upon those who had experienced the Risen Jesus (John 20:22; Acts 2:4). The gift of the Spirit was to a group of persons gathered together, and the Spirit transformed the group into a community.

In his letters, Paul suggests some aspects of this Spirit-guided community. The presence of the Spirit means the life of the Christ, the Risen Jesus (Romans 8:2-11). Life in the Spirit is the way Christians participate in the risen life of Jesus. God raised Jesus from the dead and gave the Spirit to the believers as a promise, as the first phase of their own salvation and risen life in Jesus (Romans 8:23). The gift of the Spirit is not only the yet-to-be-completed beginning of redemption, but living in the Spirit also makes believers children of God and heirs to God's reign (Romans 8:14-17). Community life in the Spirit of the

Risen Jesus is characterized by "love, joy, peace, patience, kindness, generosity, faithfulness, gentleness, self-control" (Galatians 5:22-23).

In the aftermath of the crucifixion, the Spirit of Jesus was the divine gift to the community of believers. The divine response to violence was the Spirit of patient endurance, love and peace. The divine response to the injustice of the crucifixion was to inspire a human community with the very Spirit of God. Yet today the Spirit of Jesus dwells in the community and is able to transform individuals or groups into a unity of justice, love and peace.

In the resurrection accounts, the gift of the Spirit and the gift of peace are closely linked. The constellation of new life, the Spirit of God and the peaceful ordering of things have already shown up in the creation story, in the first chapter of Genesis. Their reappearance here together in the context of the resurrection suggests nothing less than a new creation in Jesus. Jesus promises the Spirit and gives peace as a farewell gift before the death and resurrection (John 14:25-27). Later in the same Gospel, Jesus greets the fearful disciples, "Peace be with you." Then, breathing on them, Jesus says, "Receive the Holy Spirit" (John 20:21-23).

The author of Ephesians 4:1-6 reflects that the one Spirit is the origin of communal unity and that peace is that which binds the community together. Peace is a visible manifestation of the gift of the Spirit in the new creation that is the Christian community. If Jesus is the reconciliation of God, it is then consistent that the Spirit of Jesus would evidence a presence of peace and that this peace would be the peace of creation and of the end times. The God of the Risen Jesus is the Creator and the God who reigns in the new city, Jerusalem. If Jesus is the reconciliation, then it is understandable that the divine response even to violence and injustice would be peace.

Just as this Spirit was the life principle of Jesus, the incarnation and reconciliation of God, so is this Spirit of Jesus the life principle of the body of Christ now. It is in the Spirit that the disciples are the one body of Christ.[5] The believers joined by the one Spirit of Jesus are both the incarnation and the reconciliation of God in the world today. In the death and resurrection, Jesus handed over the Spirit to the community of believers, that they might be who Jesus was and that they might continue the ministry of Jesus.

Again, mention of the Spirit and peace is often connected with the ministry that Jesus passed on to the disciples. In John's Gospel, Jesus' commission to be ministers of reconciliation is joined with the blessing of peace and the gift of the Spirit (John 20:21-23). In the Gospel of Matthew, Jesus' greeting to the women on the first day of the week was "Peace." With the greeting, the Risen Jesus gave them the ministry to proclaim the good news to the eleven (Matthew 28:9-10). When Jesus encounters the eleven in Galilee, this ministry is universalized to include all nations. The Risen Jesus promises to remain with the eleven as they baptize "in the name of the Creator, and of the Son, and of the Holy Spirit" and teach the good news (Matthew 28:18-20).

In the Acts of the Apostles, the Pentecost experience of the disciples urged the proclamation of the good news of Jesus (Acts 2). In Paul's understanding, the ministries of those joined together in the one body of Christ came from the one Spirit (1 Corinthians 12:4-11; Romans 12:4-21). Throughout the Scriptures, the ministry of Jesus given to the disciples is connected with the Spirit of Jesus that they have received. The ministry of Jesus was the ministry of reconciliation.

The God of Jesus responded to the death-dealing rejection of incarnate love by inviting and in-spiriting the human persons who rejected Jesus to become who Jesus was: incarnate love and the good news of reconciliation. What a genius of human psychology! What a persistent belief in the goodness of created humanity! What an indestructible love of human persons!

4. Implications for Christian Peacemakers

People have attempted to ground their peacemaking efforts in the words of Jesus. Such an effort is less than satisfying, for a number of reasons. The first century authors of the Christian Scriptures simply did not address war and peace as a social issue, because it was not a concern.[6] It follows that the interpretation of specific texts on peace is necessarily a decontextualization from their original setting. Because war and peace were not a prime consideration in the first century, even references to peace were relatively few. In addition, the words of Jesus divorced from the person of Jesus are not able to substantiate a univocal position with regard to peace. For there are as many decontextualized references that seem more supportive of war and violence. Some examples include the statement of Jesus that he came to bring not peace but the sword (Matthew 10:34), that wars would mark the end times (Mark 13:7), and the violence in the cleansing of the temple (John 2:15).[7]

A theology of peacemaking will have firmer foundations when it is established on the person of Jesus. If Jesus is understood as the incarnation of God, as the reconciliation of God, and as the one raised by God from a violent death, then peacemaking is established as the continuation of the Jesus-event. Faith in this Jesus does have here-and-now implications for Christian living.

The ministry of Jesus was to be the incarnation of God's love accomplishing reconciliation among those estranged by sin. When Jesus handed over the Spirit to the disciples, Jesus handed over the ministry of reconciliation. Since it is vivified by the Spirit of Jesus, the Christian community not only is commissioned but also has the ability to continue the ministry of Jesus. Consequently, it can be expected that Christian peacemakers are the home of peace and reconciliation initiatives, even when they are not the cause of the disputes.

Peacemakers seek to incarnate God's response to death and violence. Living in the Spirit, peacemakers make choices that promote physical, emotional and spiritual life. Peacemakers seek responses to violence that engage the oppressor in the ministry of reconciliation. When peacemakers model themselves on Jesus, they must also expect that reconciliation will be achieved through suffering and even death. That seems to be the path historically repeated, for peace is the fundamental tension in which the peacemaker participates.

In Jesus, the reign of peace has burst into this world, but it is not yet completed. The disciple who already lives the resurrected life of Christ is not yet transformed by divinity. It is this fundamental tension that is the agony and the ecstasy of the peacemaker. The peacemaker knows the agony of possibly compromising negotiations, petty infighting and personal lapses of fidelity. But the peacemaker also knows the ecstasy of the Spirit's insights in otherwise dismal processes and in a surge of hope when the last effort has just failed miserably. Participation in this fundamental tension between the "already" and the "not yet" preserves the peacemaker from despair in the face of what remains to be done and from simplistic optimism in human potential.

Yet a final implication for the peacemaker is a reliance on a community of believers. Most obviously, persons find assurance in others when their own confidence is gone. For the Christian peacemaker, the Spirit of Jesus was given to the community gathered together, and it is in that same gathered community that the peacemaker can expect to find anew the gifts of the Spirit.

On yet another level, the completion of the reign of peace

depends on no one individual but on the whole of humanity. This has positive and negative elements to it, as the following example illustrates. A group of some 24 students read *The Challenge of Peace* in a class I was teaching. As I read their comments, I was surprised at the consistent affirmation they gave to the document. Here was a group in which peace could find a welcome reception. Yet there was the gnawing sense that the group stopped with the articulated desire for peace and had not given evidence of action on behalf of peace. One may speculate that they had not given much thought to the issue of peace prior to reading the document. Or perhaps they reflected a more or less universal desire for peace but had not yet tackled the more difficult problem of how to realize this desire in their concrete lives. Or perhaps they were not willing to put time and energy into peace activities.

These speculations do give some insight into the less positive elements of peacemaking as it involves the whole of humanity. Since peacemaking is a communal activity, it requires the cooperation of many persons. One person cannot bring about peace, for peace grows between persons and groups. But when there are large numbers of people involved, there are ample opportunities for debates on methods of peacemaking; there are people at all different stages of awareness; and there are a multitude of levels of commitment to action on behalf of peace. In spite of that, the gift of peace, the presence of the Spirit and the ministry of reconciliation were given to a community of persons.

The Jesus who is the reconciliation of God has handed over the ministry of reconciliation to the Christian community. This is not merely a nice ideal, but it is a reality awaiting incarnation in the human community.

Sister Mary Elsbernd, OSF, is an associate professor of social ethics at the Institute of Pastoral Studies, Loyola University, Chicago, and director of the Master of Divinity Program.

Notes:

1. This quotation from paragraph 22 includes the following footnote: "Cf. Second Council of Constantinople, can. 7: 'The divine Word was not changed into a human nature, nor was a human nature absorbed by the Word.' Denz. 219 (428). Cf. also Third Council of Constantinople: 'For just as His most holy and immaculate human nature, though deified, was not destroyed *(theotheisa ouk anerethe)*, but rather remained in its proper state and mode of being': Denz. 291 (556). Cf. Council of Chalcedon: 'to be acknowledged in two natures, without confusion, change, division, or separation.' Denz. 148 (302)."

2. G. M. Hopkins, "God's Grandeur," in W. H. Gardner and N.H. MacKenzie, editors, *The Poems of Gerard Manley Hopkins*, (London, 4th edition, 1967), p. 66.

3. P. Perkins, *Reading the New Testament: An Introduction* (New York/Ramsey, New Jersey, 1978), pp. 97-99, briefly states the following explanations given to Jesus' ethical teaching: literal requirements, a perfectionist ethic, an impossible ideal, archaic moral statements, demands irrelevant to the contemporary situation, fundamentally amoral world view and commands that must be rejected for a self-fulfilled life. See also J. Lambrecht, "The sayings of Jesus on nonviolence," in *Louvain Studies 12* (Winter, 1987), pages 291-305.

4. *The Challenge of Peace,* 52-54, also treats of the interrelationship of these three.

5. *The Church in the Modern World*, 22, develops this idea.

6. V. P. Furnish, "War and Peace in the New Testament," in *Interpretation 38* (October 1984) 363-379, especially 379, gives the reasons for this lack of concern as the relatively peaceful conditions in the Roman empire at this time, the lack of access to political power usually afforded minority groups and the Christian expectation that the

reign of God is coming soon.

7. G.H.C. MacGregor, *The New Testament Basis of Pacifism,* Nyack, New York 1954, chapter 2: "Does the New Testament sanction war?" interprets these and other difficult texts from a pacifist understanding.

DISTURBING THE PEACE

By Ibrahim M. Abdil-Mu'id Ramey

Does the idea of "nonviolence" imply the pursuit of peace at any cost? Does our nonviolence compel us to break with the false peace of conformity with evil and injustice, even when injustice is comfortable to us?

Most of us, I believe, become socialized and educated without any serious examination of the theory and practice of nonviolence, especially nonviolence within the context of our faith traditions and our professed love of God. We are routinely taught about the military exploits of George Washington, Ulysses Grant, and Dwight Eisenhower. But we do not learn about Mohandas Gandhi, Ghaffar Khan, Thomas Merton, or A.J. Muste or Dorothy Day, or the nonviolent martyrs who resisted the holocaust of the Nazis in the 1940s. We are not aware of the courageous examples of Christian witness against the horror of nuclear weapons and nuclear war. We are not told of the women and men of faith who, sometimes at enormous personal risk, conscientiously refused to take part in war.

We are instructed, though, that the God of the universe is a God of love, and for the most part, a God of nonviolence, somewhat in the image of a Sunday school Jesus surrounded by an adoring throng of the multiracial children of the world.

This essentially nonviolent God instructs the children, or at least the Christian-Christian ones, to abstain from killing (except for the State), stealing (except for the land and labor of "heathens"), bearing false witness, and coveting the possessions of our neighbors. This God, a perfectly orderly and just deity, ordains that true believers must be loving and kind, but also pretty much obedient to the natural social order that God has ordained. This is, I believe, the essential understanding of "peace" and nonviolence taught and transmitted by the dominant religious institutions of our society.

The idea of corporate or societal nonviolence, as a social construct, is usually associated not with justice, but rather with the absence of visible social conflict or the insurrectionary political or social movements that social conflict inevitably generates. This is the "false" nonviolence of acquiescence to injustice or oppression, undergirded by the belief that social stratification and social privilege are natural states of society, and that the "less fortunate" are the way they are, for the most part, because of their own defects of character or ability.

This sense of false nonviolence implicitly supports the social status quo. Where that status quo is associated with a particular racial, ethnic, gender or class group, the nonviolence is neither mutual nor symmetrical violence (either legal or extra-legal), is permissible as a tool of the dominant/oppressive social group(s), but it is taboo for the oppressed to use violence to overturn their oppression.

When violence is used to control or eliminate the recalcitrant "other," it is either camouflaged, or denied, or rationalized. This example is clearly evidenced in the example of the European invaders of Native America, who are historically celebrated for their use of massive violence to kill and displace untold millions of "Indians" for the noble purpose of establishing a modern nation state, while the "Indians" are denigrated as heathens and savages for their use of (far less massive) violence against these usurpers. Part of the subtext of those different views of violence is that the pilgrims and settlers and cowboys were both white and Christian, while the Native Americans were neither.

Simply put, the construct of "false" nonviolence teaches us nothing more than the passive surrender to permanent oppression. We are encouraged to believe that we live without violence if the dominant "we" lives without the threat of invasive criminal activity, turmoil in the streets, or rebellion in the institutions of the state. We are led to believe from the picture of social relationships presented by the media and other dominant social institutions, that pillage, slavery and conquest are not at the core of North American history: freedom and justice are. Violence, simply put, is not so much a part of history as it is a part of individual social aberration. Some races, and some social classes, were, by the grace of God, just better and more privileged than others: social nonviolence was simply the evidence that the "other" subordinated people went along with the arrangement and if there were troublemakers and agitators who threatened this form of "peace," the state had both the right and the obligation to use its own coercive power of violence to protect itself—and by implication, the rest of us— from these agitators.

Most church-going, law-abiding American Negroes (as we called ourselves back then) pretty much went along with this arrangement, content to grumble about racial hierarchy and Jim Crow Laws and the general rule of white supremacy, but not to challenge—except in the occasional legal sense of a challenge—this status quo. After all, we were a Christian people and a peaceful people as well, and we possessed none of the instruments of potentially violent insurrection. Besides, the parallel Negro social world of the segregated South had its own brilliantly colorful and deep culture, its own colleges and universities and churches and its own intellectual pursuits. Our "peace" was both an affirmation of self-preservation and a deferment of the struggle for true racial justice and equality.

Because the nonviolent American revolution known as the Civil Rights Movement took place, primarily, in the segregated, southern United States, and because I grew up there in the 1950s, it was natural and inevitable, that my generation would encounter the personality of Martin Luther King Jr., and become influenced by his nonviolence.

King was always represented, at least in the Negro church and in Negro public discourse, as a good and honorable man who stood up for the cause of justice and racial equality, even if his methods were judged by some as too confrontational and directly challenging to the status quo of white racial supremacy. This nonviolent movement in a collective understanding shaped by both our own fear of the power of exclusion and reprisal wielded by white people and our political disengagement of struggle against their dominant institutions, was morally right (if not always victorious) and grounded in the Christian ethos of "turning the other cheek" in the face of violence.

King's nonviolence, to us, was not so much theoretical as it was practical: since the white man had more guns and bombs, along with the means and the will to use them when necessary against recalcitrant Negroes, it only made sense to use nonviolent means in the moral and legal struggle for desegregation and civil rights. Besides, some Negro preachers and even some prominent white people, supported Dr. King.

And while I was only six years old when Rosa Parks refused to sit down in the back of that Montgomory, Alabama bus in December, 1955, the Civil Rights prairie fire, although it initially bypassed Norfolk, Virginia and much of the "upper" mid-Atlantic South, still captured the hopes, if not the engaged activist imaginations, of my own parents and my entire community. Our own segregated community, though far from affluent, was kept afloat by the post-Korean war economic expansion and the plentiful, though often unskilled, jobs generated by the Tidewater area's huge concentration of military bases. Segregation had produced both a large, black working class and underclass, and an expanding professional class of teachers, ministers and other college-educated women and men who were, in part because other opportunities simply didn't exist for them, deeply rooted in the life of our community.

Conventional wisdom suggested that our relatives in Mississippi and Alabama were dealing with a more radically racist element of white folks than those whom we had to confront. We were not on the front lines of the movement. But we prayed for Dr. King as we mourned for our family members in the deep South who were the more oppressed targets of racial animosity.

But while the world grappled with the issue of nonviolence as a legitimate tool for social liberation, an even deeper personal examination of violence crystallized in the symbolism of an object that appeared at Barraud Park in Norfolk, the segregated playground of my youth.

It was sometime in 1958, as I remember it, that a U.S. Navy Korean-War vintage jet fighter plane appeared one day on the playground to dazzle the Negro children of Norfolk. No one who I remember talking to knew where the plane came from, but I imagine that it appeared because Norfolk is, first and foremost, a "Navy town," and some people would certainly know about the fascination that kids, black and white, seem to have with war. And we, even as fairly young children, knew that America had fought a war in Korea a few years before, and won it.

So one day this huge, blue, winged thing appeared, and we would scramble up a little ladder to sit in its stripped, open cockpit, or crawl through the tailpipe, or play as if the machine guns and rocket pods on the wings were still there. Vaguely aware that some black men had taken to the air to do battle against Hitler's Luftwaffe in the "good" World War II, we little, black boys could fire at imaginary enemy Migs or drop imaginary bombs on Chinese and Korean communists and kill them, righteously, for America.

Something did bother me about the fighter plane in the play-ground, even though, as a Boy Scout, I was getting subtle but clear indoctrination in the glories of the war system. After all, didn't the Sunday School Jesus tell us not to kill? And if He did tell us not to kill, wouldn't the commandment equally apply to people who kill in war?

My church pastor, the venerable, fiery Dr. Henry T. Myers, never questioned the legitimacy of this instrument of war on a segregated, Southern playground. I recall no sermons that examined the question of the morality of armed violence in North American history, or how the war system imposed any disproportionate burden upon the black and the poor.

While the fighter plane eventually left Barraud Park, it was not until 1967 when, as a high school senior with deeply ambivalent feelings about the war in Vietnam, I listened to Dr. King's speech at Riverside Church condemning the war and the role of organizad violence in the entire context of American history. Dr. King's great leap forward into the ranks of antiwar activism was a profound threat to the false "peace" of complicity with the military status quo and the war system that my generation was in in Indochina. It was then that I began to develop the understanding that nonviolence is not a passive resistance to racism: it is an active resistance to war. Kingian nonviolence opened the door to examine much more than legalized segregation and the mistreatment of black people in the South; it compelled its students and followers to rigorously examine the content and character not only of our own hearts, but of every institution of our society, as well. Even the United States military, the huge engine of our local Tidewater economy and the upholder of freedom and democracy throughout the world, was an essentially violent institution completely outside the just boundaries of the "Beloved Community." My church upbringing, and even my elevation to the Boy Scout rank of Eagle

Scout at the age of sixteen, left me unprepared for looking at my own role as either a potential victim of organized violence, or as one of its future perpetrators.

But there is a another lesson learned from the war images of my childhood playground and the turbulent struggle of Dr. King's social movement. It is the lesson that nonviolence, far from being passive resistance, is a powerful tool of social analysis and a yardstick to measure not only our own hearts, but in a larger sense, the immorality and injustice imbedded in our unexamined social institutions.

The nonviolence of Martin Luther King Jr. was, and is, an evolving ideology of love and resistance, a dialectical and unfolding idea rooted in the ahimsa ("harmlessness in thought, word, and deed") of Mohandas Gandhi and the theological construction of the American Christian theologian Walter Raustenbusch, who believed that the logical conclusion of nonviolence was the bringing forth of nothing less than the "Beloved Community" of God, a human community where human differences were both respected and tolerated, and where the material well-being and human dignity of all of its members would be guaranteed. This Kingian nonviolence opposes both racial hostility and oppression, in the sense that it rejects both acts of individual harm and the more entrenched forms of institutional racism and intolerance, with the power of love and organized, unarmed resistance. This nonviolence embraces peace. But instead of the mere absence of armed conflict or the peace imposed by political compromise or military conquest, it strives for a permanent peace of the collective heart and soul of the nation, and the world, that is rooted in abiding and absolute justice.

And this real, God-centered gospel of nonviolence is holistic. It does not say that only racism and war are evil; it challenges the deeper, more entrenched reality of class oppression and poverty. Martin Luther King's challenge to the American nation was also, essentially, a challenge to the ethos of capitalism itself. Kingian nonviolence declared that capitalism, to the extent that it was built upon the enslavement of Africans and the exploitation of countless others, is itself a system that opposed spiritual and social justice. Because even if there is no war and no racial strife, the nonviolence of Martin Luther King informed us that the economic subjugation of the poor (and the working class) by the rich was, in itself, a form of violence. This meant, at least to me, that the system of capitalism (even the "black" variety of capitalism that would be pushed a few years later by the Nixon administration), despite its cool, glittery facade of comfortable consumerism, is based on principles of entrenched violence and exploitation.

Nonviolence is not for the intellectually weak or the cowardly. It is not for those who wish to only avoid confrontation or who seek to quietly and comfortably coexist with violent and unjust institutions as long as our own discomfort is minimized. Nonviolence is even sometimes emotionally painful, because in its own relentless search for truth, it compels us, out of spiritual and moral honesty, to question, and even separate ourselves from otherwise comfortable personal relationships that are undergirded by complicity with violence and injustice.

The nonviolence of Martin Luther King is a lighthouse that illuminates the struggle for a world that is free of racial injustice, poverty and war. It is both a method useful to deconstruct the false notion that "peace can be removed from real justice, and that power can only exist within the context of hierarchy and inequality." This nonviolence compels us to re-examine and reconstruct our history, our cultural and racial assumptions, and most of all, our allegiances.

Nonviolence does disturb the peace. It disturbs the peace of silent complicity with unjust institutions and actions, even when we believe that they do not directly affect us. It disturbs the "peace" of materialistic self-indulgence and the "peace" of disengagement from the struggle for human liberation. It disturbs the "peace" of false history, and a false sense of racial or class superiority. It even disturbs the "peace" of the oppressed people who seek quiet assimilation into the marginal comforts of the systems that dominate them.

I, for one, am happy that the vision and the courage of Dr. Martin Luther King disturbed my peace as a young man. Because now I can declare my own allegiance to the struggle for the Beloved Community, and for a world where my children and their children will never go to poor, segregated playgrounds to play on the wings of war-planes.

Ibrahim M. Abdil-Mùid Ramey, the current peace and disarmament program coordinator of the Fellowship of Reconciliation, is a native of Norfolk, Va. and a resident of New York City.

Ramey's work with the peace and justice community began when, after a trip to North Korea as a delegate to an anti-nuclear peace conference, he joined the national staff of the War Resisters League. After a one-year hiatus to develop special projects for the Youth Action Program in East Harlem, Ramey accepted his current position with FOR. Ramey has spoken and conducted workshops on social justice issues throughout the United States, Africa and Asia. His essays have appeared in The Nonviolence Activist, Fellowship *maga-zine,* Peace News, *and the* Syracuse Peace Journal.

THE PROBLEM OF PEACE AND JUSTICE IN EVOLUTIONARY PERSPECTIVE

By Rev. Richard Viladesau

In his early and now classic series of robot stories, science fiction author Isaac Asimov imagines a future time in which humanity constructs anthropoid robots that far surpass their makers in both intelligence and strength. To assure that such formidable servants never become a threat to their human inventors, an unbreakable program of behavior is implanted in their circuits. Its most fundamental and absolute principle is the "first law of robotics," which commands: "A robot may not injure a human being nor, through inactivity, allow a human being to come to harm."

Robots thus become totally benevolent and highly efficient promoters of human welfare. But in his later "Foundation" series of novels, Asimov invents an unforeseen development. A super-intelligent robot, capable of independent thought, realizes that the two parts of the "first law" can come into conflict: Obedience to the first part would sometimes involve disobedience to the second; avoidance of the sin of commission would sometimes involve a much greater sin of omission.

Like the surgeon who amputates a gangrenous limb, the robot first reasons that in order to prevent greater harm to human beings, it is sometimes necessary to inflict lesser harm; by analogy, it reasons that in order not to allow harm to come to a greater number, it can sometimes be necessary to harm individuals; and, finally, in order to avoid injury to humanity in the long run, it may sometimes be necessary to allow or even inflict it in the present.

Science fiction, of course, is generally not about science; it is a

73

reflection on the problems of living in human community. The dilemma faced by Asimov's robot in some ways parallels the intellectual and moral problems encountered in religious thought about warfare that were factors in the formation of various theories of the "just war."

The religious motivation of "just war" theory

As historian John Keegan remarks, the great monotheistic religions (and even more, one might add, the non-theistic religions of Jainism and Buddhism) condemn the killing of fellow human beings "in all but the most constrained circumstances,"[2] and therefore have been a major force in promoting peace and opposing warfare.[3] When the concept of a tribal or local god is replaced with that of a transcendent and universal Absolute (whether conceived theistically or not), the correlative concept of the universal brotherhood and sisterhood of humankind naturally follows.[4] This in turn implies a "golden rule" of ethics and even an imperative to some kind of universal goodness, conceived with differing emphases as love, benevolence, or compassion.

Nevertheless, the "transcendental" religions have seldom extended their ethical code to include a complete condemnation of violence or warfare under all circumstances. The reason is a dilemma similar to that of Asimov's beneficent robot: The love of neighbor demands not only refraining from harm, but actively pursuing justice. In a world already infected with sin, manifest as conflict and violence,[5] an active pursuit of goodness sometimes seems to demand the use of force to stop or to eliminate evil. Love of neighbor demands not merely good wishes, but effective action; the omission of such action is just as immoral as the commission of evil. Hence, it is argued, to allow our neighbor to suffer unjust violence and to refrain from opposing it by effective means—by force, if that is the only effective means—would be inconsistent with real love of either the victim or the aggressor. It would be in effect to allow that unjust violence, to collaborate with it, even perhaps to encourage it.

Thus, along with exhortations of non-resistance to evil have appeared religious and theological justifications of self-defense and even of righteous warfare, either as a response to aggression or as a pursuit of justice. So, for example, God in the Qur'an demands not only personal but also societal engagement for justice, and expostulates with the faithful who do not wish to engage in battle: "How could you refuse to fight in the way of Allah and on behalf of the weak... and those who cry out, 'O Lord'?"[6] Primary among theological justifications of limited uses of armed force in the modern world is the Christian theological exposition of the criteria for a "just war."[7]

The critique of "just war" theory

The theological theory of the "just war" has been subjected to increasing theological criticism in recent years, partly in reaction to an explicit appeal to it in the justification of the Gulf War.[8] Three categories used by Jesuit moralist John P. Langan are helpful in classifying the major forms of opposition to the theory.[9] The strict pacifist position holds that war is always wrong, and that "just war" theory is fundamentally incompatible with either general human or specifically Christian values. The "incompleteness" objection holds that the theory leaves out of consideration certain aspects either of warfare in general or of warfare as practiced in the contemporary world, and therefore does not apply to current situations. The "indeterminacy" objection points out that the theory, while perhaps not incorrect in principle, is not useful in practice, because it contains too many complex elements to allow one to draw a clear conclusion about actual cases. (One might join to these the objection that the "just war" theory can be and has been misused to provide a rationalization that disguises the true motives for war-making that in reality serves other interests than "justice."[10] Logically, this is an objection to the application of the theory rather than to the theory itself;[11] a supporter of the theory could equally admit to the possibility or actuality of its misuse. Hence this objection, insofar as it is directed against "just war" theory itself, is perhaps best seen as an extension of one or more of those mentioned above, pointing out their practical consequence.)

At first sight, the three categories of objections may seem radically different. The pacifist position seems to lead to rejection of the theory of "just war" itself, while the other two might be seen to call rather for its improvement or expansion. In fact, however, the objections are often mixed, and there appears to be a good deal of overlapping of concerns.

Pacifism in practice is frequently "relative" rather than absolute. That is, there are those who oppose warfare in general, or are pacifist in disposition or in hope, but who are unwilling to make an absolute and universal judgment on the matter. They leave room, on the theoretical level, for exceptions. (I have several older friends, for example, who characterize themselves as lifelong pacifists, but who nevertheless considered it a moral duty to fight against Hitler's aggressions.)

On the other hand, the "incompleteness" and "indeterminacy" objections can be "absolutely" pacifist if they are taken to point either to intrinsic limitations of the theory that cannot be overcome on a theoretical level, or even to intrinsic limitations of theoretical understanding itself. Even if they are only directed at the re-examination and "improvement" of the theory, they are compatible with "relative" pacifism. For, as Langan points out, the "just war" theory operates with a strong presumption against war,[12] and those who hold it may find its usefulness precisely in setting conditions that cannot possibly be met in practice.

Complications of the contemporary situation

A further dimension of complexity is added to the discussion by the political and social realities of the post-Cold War world. Contemporary situations challenge traditional formulations of both "just war" theory and pacifism, whether universal or modified. Increasingly, the world community has had to attend to armed conflicts that are not "warfare" between nation-states, but are the expression of internal strife: rebellions against unjust living conditions, competition for scarce resources, tribal and ethnic animosities, et cetera. The notions of "humanitarian intervention," "police action," and even "peacekeeping" and "peacemaking" have been applied to the use of armed force by outside powers in such conflicts.[13]

In Somalia, United Nations and United States troops were used to enforce an end to tribal violence that was not only causing widespread starvation, but also blocking humanitarian efforts to counter it. Proponents of such intervention point out that the threat (and sometimes the use) of armed force saved hundreds of thousands of innocent lives. On the other hand, in Rwanda the international community refused to intervene militarily, despite desperate and heartrending pleas from the victims of aggression. In Bosnia, intervention came only after months of destructive conflict and "ethnic cleansing" had horrified the world.

From the beginnings of each of these conflicts, proponents of military intervention have argued that the use of outside force—or possibly even the mere threat of force—would have prevented the much greater evils that took place in the absence of intervention. Even those who disagree cannot but be moved by the victims' appeal to the world's conscience. Have the great powers and the United Nations, by refusing effective action, implicitly consented to genocide, as victims have claimed? For the Christian conscience concerned with peace and justice, the question is an agonizing one, because the anguished question of the suffering—"Why haven't you stopped this horror?"—evokes the Gospel admonition: "Whatever you failed to do for these least ones, you failed to do for me" (Matthew 25:45).[14]

Theological and moral issues: the contribution of evolutionary theory

The discussion of the morality of the use of force under the rationale either of "just war" or of "humanitarian intervention" and the relation of these to the ideal of Christian pacifism raises many theological and practical questions that are beyond the scope of this article and the competence of its author. My intention here is a modest one. As Langan points out, "just war" theorists and their opponents have a great deal of moral ground in common and frequently share "an intense commitment to justice and the transformation of society."[15] All agree that peace is to be sought and that war is an evil.

My intention is to "bracket" the irreconcilable differences between the "absolute" pacifist position that all warfare, under whatever name, is always wrong, and the "realist" just-war/just-intervention position that armed conflict is an evil, but sometimes a lesser evil. I shall concentrate instead on the proposition that the pacifist view, whether it is at present "realistic" or not, should become increasingly true: that is, that humanity can and should be constructing a world in which it is never reasonable or responsible for communities to resort to violence, even in response to violence.[16]

My proposal is to look at this progression toward peace in the perspective of evolution. In the following considerations, which must remain a mere outline, I will suggest that:

1) Contemporary anthropology and sociobiology give us insights into underlying causes of human violence and indicate that there are

conditions for overcoming them.

2) A philosophical view that takes into account this sociobiological perspective allows us to view moral perspectives, including those regarding warfare, as subject to a kind of evolution on the cultural level.

3) Consequently, there are specific material and spiritual conditions of possibility for the emergence of nonviolence as a universal and realizable moral option.

4) These conditions suggest areas that must be addressed by those who are committed to forwarding peace.

Sociobiological factors

Contemporary anthropology, drawing on insights not only from biology, history and sociology, but also from genetics and neurology, offers limited but significant perspectives on human propensities toward conflict. There is general agreement that evolution has to some extent genetically predisposed human beings to aggressive and violent behavior, at least in some situations. Sharp disagreements remain, however, concerning the relative importance of different factors in influencing human conduct: heredity vs. environment, material vs. cultural factors, "lower" vs. "higher" brain control. The most pessimistic scientists argue the minority opinion that humanity is naturally and unalterably violent. The majority holds that although aggressive behavior may be genetically programmed into our "lower" brain functions, nevertheless environmental circumstances, which are to some extent within human control, are crucial in determining human reactions.[17]

The views of Harvard sociobiologist Edward O. Wilson represent the more optimistic position. We must admit, according to

Wilson, that human beings are innately aggressive. "Throughout history, warfare, representing only the most organized technique of aggression, has been endemic to every form of society, from hunter-gatherer bands to industrial states....Only by redefining the words 'innateness' and 'aggression' to the point of uselessness might we correctly say human aggressiveness is not innate....Human beings have a marked hereditary predisposition to aggressive behavior."[18]

Wilson's studies lead him to conclude that "we are strongly predisposed to slide into deep, irrational hostility under certain definable conditions."[19] Wilson adds: "Human beings are strongly predisposed to respond with unreasoning hatred to external threats and to escalate their hostility sufficiently to overwhelm the source of the threat by a respectably wide margin of safety. Our brains do appear to be programmed to the following extent: we are inclined to partition other people into friends and aliens....We tend to fear deeply the actions of strangers and to solve conflict by aggression. These learning rules are most likely to have evolved during the past hundreds of thousands of years of human evolution and, thus, to have conferred a biological advantage on those who conformed to them with the greatest fidelity."[20] Wilson hastens to point out, however, that "innateness," from a scientific point of view, does not mean inevitability. It refers "to the measurable probability that a trait will develop in a specified set of environments, not to the certainty that the trait will develop in all environments."[21]

The evolutionary advantage that aggressive behavior confers in the struggle for physical survival applies to groups as well as individuals. Hence, although specific forms of aggressive behavior, like warfare, are learned, not inborn, the ability and disposition to learn them form part of our genetic inheritance. Furthermore, according to Wilson, the "evolution of warfare was an autocatalytic reaction that could not be halted by any people, because to attempt to reverse the process unilaterally was to fall victim."[22]

At the same time, it must be emphasized that for Wilson and most of his colleagues, the disposition to aggressive or violent behavior is neither exclusive nor all-determinative. It is one of the genetic influences on conduct. Humans are also genetically predisposed to collaboration and to altruism (although usually within fairly strict limits).[23] Which dispositions become active depends largely upon circumstances, and circumstances are increasingly within the realm of human choice. Hence, Wilson holds out the hope that humanity can direct its inherited impulses. "Although the evidence suggests that the biological nature of humankind launched the evolution of organized aggression and roughly directed its early history across many societies, the eventual outcome of that evolution will be determined by cultural processes brought increasingly under the control of rational thought."[24]

Evolution and emergent probability

If the insights of sociobiology lead to the hope that human behavior is not simply at the mercy of deterministic biological inheritance, but depends—to some extent—on human circumstances and choices, then another form of evolution becomes important to our discussion: the evolution of cultures, in which values are enshrined and by which (within limits) human circumstances are created. That evolution may be seen as a special case of what philosopher and theologian Bernard Lonergan calls "emergent probability."[25.]

The notion of emergent probability is based on a simple insight. Evolution involves "chance." That is, it depends upon the occurrence of events or circumstances that are not ubiquitous or inevitable. They do not occur universally, and when they do occur, it is because certain enabling conditions are present. "Chance" is not totally indeterminate; the probability of the occurrence of any event or circumstance arises out of prior contexts that both provide and limit possibilities. The chances for the occurrence and survival of any pattern of events or activities (for example, the development of the more complex forms of life) are not the same always and everywhere. They emerge out of the establishment of prior conditions, such as the prior development of simpler forms of life in which mutations can take place. The chance for this development in turn depends upon the prior emergence of organic compounds, and so forth.

"Emergent probability" thus provides an understanding of an open and evolutionary world process, avoiding the extremes of both determinism and indeterminism. In the development of the actual world we observe an increasingly systematic character: Higher and more complex levels of existence emerge out of lower and simpler ones, at the cost of the expenditure of energy. The development of more complex schemes and forms of life depends on variations occurring in earlier patterns and providing some advantage. At the same time, the process admits breakdowns: Any pattern of events has only a probability of survival, given the right conditions. Since earlier patterns provide the conditions for later ones, the breakdown of the former involves the breakdown of the latter. (So, for example, human culture depends upon natural ecosystems; if the environment is destroyed, so is civilization.) The process also permits blind alleys: Some developments that have a high probability of survival will for that very reason have little possibility of change. (Sharks, for example, remain comparatively unevolved because they are so well adapted.[26])

Emergent probability and cultural evolution

According to Lonergan, the "conditions of emergence and survival of modes of living"—that is, of human culture—also follow the more general pattern of emergent probability.[27] Of course, humans' physical and spiritual lives depend upon the emergence and survival of the appropriate material and biological cycles that provide the conditions for life and thought. But there is also a further level. Humanity both affects the physical world and builds its own "spiritual" world of meanings and values. As the "humanization" of the world occurs, human survival and development depend increasingly on humanity's own contribution, and "more and more importance attaches to the probabilities of the occurrence of insight, communication, agreement, decision."[28] Instead of merely being developed by an environment, humanity—although never completely in control—increasingly transforms the environment into the instrument of humanity's own development.[29]

The occurrence of the human contribution, however, is neither automatic nor purely random; it emerges from prior conditions. Some of these conditions are material: the basic "necessities of life," to begin with, but also such things as health, leisure, freedom from constant struggle for survival, et cetera. Others are psychological, societal and cultural. In order to make intelligent and responsible decisions, people must be able to grasp the data; must have a language and concepts adequate to thinking and communicating about them; must be able to envision appropriate options; must be able to see such options as reasonable and responsible and desirable. The probability of a positive human response to situations will depend upon the presence or absence of these conditions, and this will in turn depend largely upon prior human insights and decisions, or the lack of them. "What possesses a high probability in one country, or period, or civilization, may possess no probability in another; and the ground of the difference may lie only slightly in outward and palpable material factors and almost entirely in the set of insights that are accessible, persuasive, and potentially operative in the community."[30]

The failures of cultural evolution

Unfortunately, increased "humanization" of the world also means that the lack of intelligent and responsible action has more dire effects. The absence or the disregard of timely ideas, insights, perspectives, collaborations, not only excludes their implementation—thus eliminating further progress that would build on them—but also undermines much of what has already been achieved, so that the social situation deteriorates cumulatively.[31] Thus there is not only cultural evolution, but also cultural decline. "In this fashion social functions and enterprises begin to conflict; some atrophy and others grow like tumors; the objective situation becomes penetrated with anomalies...."[32] Lonergan calls such structural evils the "social surd," adding that "the social situation is the cumulative product of individual and group decisions, and as these decisions depart from the demands of intelligence and reasonableness, so the social situation becomes, like the complex number, a compound of the rational and irrational."[33] The result is that there are elements in the human situation that are "objectively" unintelligible, that have no sufficient reason for being, and that can evoke no rational response except their reversal.

In Lonergan's perspective, aggression and violence among people may be seen to have several levels of causation. They result from animal instincts that have not been integrated into a higher level of the human good; they stem from incomplete visions of that good, such as egotism or group or national bias; they are an inadequate attempt to overcome the social surd. The use of force, however, does not solve the human problem; rather, it treats the problem as insoluble. "Only in the measure that [people] are unintelligent, unreasonable, unwilling, does force enter into human affairs."[34]

The solution to this problem cannot consist in the discovery of the correct philosophy or ethics or religion; for "precisely because they are correct, they will not appear correct to minds disorientated by the conflict between positions and counterpositions. Precisely because they are correct, they will not appear workable to wills with restricted ranges of effective freedom. Precisely because they are correct, they will be weak competitors for serious attention in the realm of practical affairs."[35] The only possible solution, for Lonergan, is a "higher integration" of human living by God's grace.

Christian morality in an evolutionary view of the world

Christians believe that God has in fact offered humanity a new and "higher" synthesis of existence through grace. But this "solution" does not replace human responsibility, for the integration itself comes to humanity through an emergent probability of human realization, acceptance, and collaboration. The font of Christian morality is the gift of the "love of God flooding our hearts," opening our minds and wills to the absolute love of God and neighbor. But interior conversion is not sufficient, nor does it provide a "shortcut" that can evade the need for intelligent reasoning on exactly what constitutes "love of neighbor" in the complexities of a world already infected with sin and the social surd. As Lonergan says: "One can agree with Christian praise of charity....But good will is never better than the intelligence and reasonableness that it implements. Indeed, when proposals and programmes only putatively are intelligent and reasonable then the good will that executes them so faithfully and energetically is engaged really in the systematic imposition of ever further evils on the already weary shoulders of mankind (sic)."[36]

God's word and God's love are understood and made active in accord with varying human possibilities for understanding and expressing them; these possibilities both express and limit the divine dynamism in us. Hence, there is a necessary dialectic between two levels that Rosemary Luling Haughton has called "transformation," or being "converted" to the absolute love of God, and "formation," or the developing human self-understandings, meanings, concepts, judgments and values that constitute a person's world, and in which conversion takes place. "Transformation is a timeless point of decision, yet it can only operate in the personality formed through time-conditioned stages of development, and its effects can only be worked out in terms of that formation."[37]

Transformation is limited in two ways. "It is limited by the type of formation a person has had, and in practice this means the kind of language in which he (sic) has learned to understand what he (sic) is and work out what he (sic) is. And it is limited by the language in which the person he (sic) is understands the offer of salvation, and responds to it."[38] Haughton uses the case of Joan of Arc to exemplify a transformation experience of intense love of God worked out in a limited conversion "language" that saw God's will as warfare against the enemies of France. Such limitation by the horizons of the human recipient of grace is unavoidable. "This does not mean that the transformation is not genuine. It simply means that the area of living affected by it depends entirely on the kind of personal language in which the converting encounter is expressed."[39]

On such an understanding it is clear that the Christian moral vision of love will also be involved in an evolutionary dynamic of emergent probability. The imperative of loving activity is always "an incomplete set of insights that is ever to be completed differently in each concrete situation."[40] In a world that is incomplete, evolving, and partially formed by free decisions, it must be so, for concrete courses of action are always complex configurations of values and disvalues. There is seldom a choice of total right or wrong; most frequently we are faced with a choice of higher or lower goods that are inseparable from some greater or lesser evils. The Christian's social task will consist in making higher and more universal realizations of love increasingly possible and probable by helping to create the "formational" conditions—material, cultural and spiritual—in which they can be realized in individuals and communities.

The emergent probability of peace

If we accept Lonergan's account of natural and cultural evolution, as well as the findings of contemporary anthropology, it is obvious that peace among people is not equally possible as a practical or a moral option at every time and under every circumstance. Its probability, however, can emerge through human development. The "just war" theories that were developed in the great religions represented a step in that evolution, in that they replaced the presumption that warfare is simply a natural state of affairs with the contention that it can only be justified by extraordinary circumstances.

The emergence of a further level, in which violence is renounced altogether, would seem to depend upon establishing its conditions of possibility on three different but interrelated levels. The necessary sociobiological condition for nonviolence is that human agents have advanced beyond the level of instinctual behavior to that of free choice and control. The necessary ethical condition is that nonviolence both be and be perceived as a rational and responsible reaction to conflictual social situations, including already existent aggression. The necessary spiritual condition is that people accept God's grace forming the will to love rationally and responsibly.

The fulfilling of these conditions is not merely a matter of chance, as in natural evolution, but is (at least in part) a result of human purpose. That is to say, it is possible for us consciously to direct the emergence of probabilities toward the good. The "innateness" of violent behavior at the biological level and its justification on the ethical level are tied to circumstances. If certain circumstances arise, a violent response is natural and probable because of our genetic inheritance; if certain circumstances arise, forceful opposition to aggression may be the most reasonable and probable moral reaction. But such circumstances need not arise—in particular on the second level, where by definition they are themselves undesirable, irrational, and immoral. Peace becomes an emergent probability, to the extent that we can reverse or mitigate conditions that lead to conflict, develop those that promote collaboration, and create means of dealing with the failures of both efforts.

Such efforts toward peace must perforce operate on many levels and in many areas. An important element is an understanding of the complexity of the problem. John Keegan wrote his *History of Warfare* to show that the common modern understanding of warfare, based on Clausewitz, is wrong: War is not simply the continuation of politics by other means.[41] If we misunderstand it in this way, we will miss many of its true causes and fruitlessly espouse political solutions to largely non-political problems. In particular, we must advert to the connection of warfare with the unsystematic violence of crime and the systematic violence of structural evils of oppression in societies.

"If you want peace, work for justice." The United States bishops have adopted this phrase from Pope Paul VI as the slogan of their Campaign for Human Development. Those who work for peace have long recognized the connection between conflict and the "social surd," particularly dehumanizing poverty and institutional violence. We are becoming increasingly aware of its connection with other factors, such as the pollution of the biosphere.[42]

The title of a much discussed article by Robert D. Kaplan catalogues some of the interrelated problems leading to strife: "The coming anarchy: how scarcity, crime, overpopulation, tribalism, and disease are rapidly destroying the social fabric of our planet."[43] Kaplan argues that future wars will increasingly be like the struggles already taking place in parts of Africa, where the distinction between warfare, crime and ethnic conflict has broken down. In the competition for survival on ever scarcer resources, the problems of overpopulation, environmental degradation, and interracial or intercultural hostility merge together. Such analyses raise the specter of a "dialectic of decline," in which the prospects for peaceful resolutions decrease rather than becoming more probable, and in which the dilemma of Asimov's beneficent robot again comes to the fore.

If, instead, peace is to become realizable for humanity as a whole, it can only be through our consciously creating the conditions necessary for its possibility to emerge. This implies fundamental changes in human attitudes and situations, and not only among the Third World peoples who are most threatened by violence. Among other things, it demands of the prosperous nations of the world a sense of responsibility for overcoming the sources of conflicts. The pursuit of this topic leads beyond the bounds of the present discussion. But it seems clear, for example, that material poverty and its social and environmental consequences within Third World nations constitute a major source of conflicts, and that the policies of more prosperous nations can have a direct positive or negative effect on our poorer neighbors. On the other hand, the prosperous countries must recover a meaning of human well-being that is not purely material.

Obviously, Christianity and the other world religions have a great deal to contribute to the realization of such goals. In addition to images of the horrors of war, they must provide images of justice and peace that are attractive and persuasive, even though they involve self-sacrifice. The challenge is a large one, and the courage to face it can only be based on the conviction that God's Spirit is in fact operative among us, among all people, expanding our minds and inspiring our hearts.

Rev. Richard Viladesau, a priest of the Diocese of Rockville Centre, teaches theology at Fordham University in The Bronx, New York. He is the author of Theological Aesthetics *(Oxford University*

Press, 1999), and two books to be published by Paulist Press in 2000:
Theology and the Arts *and a collection of his Christmas and Easter homilies, the last in a series called* The World In and Out of Season.

Notes:

1. An expanded version of this article, including a more extensive treatment of the various forms of pacifism, appears in the *Journal for Peace and Justice Studies of Villanova University*, Vol. 7, No. 1 (1996), pp. 13-52.

2. John Keegan: *A History of Warfare* (New York: Alfred A. Knopf, 1993), p. 3.

3. It is easy, of course, to find exceptions to this generalization. When combined with tribal or nationalistic cultures, monotheistic religion can tolerate or even promote conflict. Thus, the God of the Exodus commands the Hebrew people to engage in an aggressive war of appropriation of the land of Canaan, and is frequently invoked as a god of war; the greatest sacred book of theistic Hinduism, the *Bhagavad-Gita*, sanctions warfare as a caste duty; Christianity, despite early tendencies to pacifism, adapted to warrior cultures and eventually initiated crusades against nonbelievers; Islam's *Qur'an* explicitly commands holy warfare against the "enemies of God," and the normative example of Muhammad established the practice; even generally nonviolent Buddhism developed orders of warrior monks, and its principles were involved in the fighting code of Bushido.

4. Naturally, one can also enumerate many instances of religious failures to observe this principle; the most obvious, perhaps, regards the treatment of women.

5. The realities referred to throughout this essay with the terms "conflict," "violence," "aggression," "warfare," et cetera, have many dimensions. It is to be understood that I am using them here in the context of armed conflict between communities or nations. Likewise,

terms like "nonviolence" are not used absolutely, but in the sense of the abjuration of such communal combat.

6. Surah IV, 75.

7. The theory of the "just war," as developed in Christian theology, has interesting parallels in the Islamic tradition. Muslim jurists have tended to impose restrictive conditions on the practice of jihad or "holy war," which, in theory, can only be waged on nonbelievers. Many pious Muslims have interpreted the *Qur'an's* injunctions in terms of "spiritual" warfare.

8. See, for example, John P. Langan, S.J.: "The Just War Theory after the Gulf War" in *Theological Studies*, Vol. 53, No. 1 (March 1992), pp. 95-112.

9. Langan, p. 99. I am here summarizing Langan's exposition of the three objections, while expanding on certain points.

10. Langan notes that this is a point made in the editorial "Coscienza cristiana e guerra moderna" in *La Civiltà Cattolica* 142 (1991), pp. 3-16.

11. Indeed, a "hermeneutic of suspicion"—the notion that a particular intellectual position is a rational or rhetorical structure that covers over hidden agendas—can be applied to any idea or mental construct whatsoever. Marx used it to argue —with some plausibility—against religion. But religious people can admit that religion sometimes masks ungodly attitudes (they may indeed point to the critiques of "false" religion engaged in by the Jewish prophets and by Jesus) without concluding that religion itself should be abandoned. One might equally apply a hermeneutic of suspicion to Marxism, or pacifism, or to hermeneutical suspicion itself. Any discourse, including the most rational and virtuous, can be used as an "ideology" to justify behavior "really" based on other, hidden motives. Hence, to claim that "just war" theory is in fact being so (mis)used is a significant and valid ad

hominem argument; but it does not per se touch the validity of the theory itself.

12. Langan, p. 103.

13. For a survey of the discussion of moral norms for such actions, see Kenneth R. Himes, O.F.M.: "The Morality of Humanitarian Intervention" in *Theological Studies* Vol. 55, No. 1 (March 1994), pp. 82-105.

14. These remarks are not meant to be an argument in favor of intervention, which is opposed even by many non-pacifists on a number of grounds, including the crucial one that intervention would not in fact end the conflict, but would prolong and intensify it. The point here is merely to illustrate the complexity of the problem of conscience.

15. Langan, p. 100.

16. I will also prescind from the question of whether such a world is actually attainable or is a "utopian" ideal that can only be approached asymptotically. This question obviously overlaps with the theological debate over the relation of human effort to the "Kingdom" of God. Even if one takes the position that Karl Rahner calls "Christian pessimism" about the world, the approach itself remains a legitimate and morally necessary effort.

17. Keegan, pp. 79ff.

18. Edward O. Wilson: *On Human Nature* (Cambridge, Mass.: Harvard University Press, 1978), p. 99f.

19. Wilson, p. 106.

20. Wilson, p. 119. Cf. Keegan, p. 82: "aggressiveness is clearly a genetic inheritance that may enhance the chance of survival."

21. Wilson, p. 100.

22. Wilson, p.116.

23. Wilson, pp. 149-167. On collaboration, see also Richard E. Leakey: *The Making of Mankind* (New York: E. P. Dutton, 1981), p. 242.

24. Wilson, p. 116.

25. Bernard J. F. Lonergan, S.J.: *Insight: A Study of Human Understanding* (New York: Philosophical Library, 1957), p. 121ff. Lonergan's definition of "emergent probability" as a property of the world process as a whole is: "the successive realization in accord with successive schedules of probability of a conditioned series of schemes of recurrence" (p. 125f.).

26. Lonergan, pp. 126ff.

27. Lonergan, p. 124. We may see here an echo of Teilhard de Chardin's insight into the continuity between biological and spiritual evolution. Liberation theologian Juan Luis Segundo develops a somewhat similar line of thought in his discussion of entropy and negentropy.

28. Lonergan, p 210.

29. Insight, p. 227.

30. Lonergan, p. 211.

31. Insight, p. 229.

32. Insight, p. 229

33. Insight, p. 628.

34. Insight, p. 632.

35. Insight, p. 632.

36. Lonergan, p. 629. Lonergan's position is in line with that of St. Thomas, for whom love cannot exist without the other virtues, "through which we accomplish specific kinds of good works" (*Summa Theologica II, I*, q. 65, a. 3). Love is the "form" of the virtues, ordering them to their final end; but is not their "material" cause (*S.T. II, II*, q. 24, a.8). Hence, one cannot truly be virtuous without using practical reasoning and understanding to know in the concrete what is the "loving" course of action (*S.T. II, II*, q. 47, a. 14; I, II, q. 58, a. 4).

37. Haughton, Rosemary: *The Transformation of Man* (New York: Paulist Press, 1967), p. 32.

38. Haughton, p. 137.

39. Haughton, p. 137. Note that one cannot avoid this limitation by appealing, for example, to the formation language of the New Testament, because 1) it also is formulated in and limited by a culturally conditioned context; 2) it is itself complex and non-systematic; 3) it does not cover every aspect of human conduct, and therefore must be "applied" to situations it does not foresee; 4) there is no appropriation without interpretation, which will again depend upon the "formation"—the horizons and presuppositions—of the interpreter.

40. Lonergan, p. 211.

41. Keegan, p. 3.

42. Wilson notes that "most kinds of aggressive behavior among members of the same species are responsive to crowding in the environment" (p. 103).

43. In *The Atlantic Monthly* Vol. 273 (Feb. 1994), pp. 44-76.

Jubilee: A Catechesis for "Being Peace"

By Maria Harris

In January of 1991, the day after Operation Desert Storm started,
Padraic O'Hare walked into his religious studies classroom in North
Andover, Massachusetts.[1] He was tempted, he reports, to discuss the
onset of the Gulf War, in order to see what the students were thinking
and how they were reacting. But on second thought, he asked the class
to pray. Their praying would not be an attempt at magical manipula-
tion of the divine, he explained. A God who could have prevented
Desert Storm would have done so.

Instead, he suggested they pray because prayer can make us
attentive, mindful. Prayer can make us pause, can slow us down, can
assist us in "thick" listening. Prayer is, or can be, a special kind of
awareness, for if and when we pray—with the eyes and heart of a bod-
dhisattva—we become cognizant we are all implicated in any action
taken by even a single one of us. Human, we belong to a species in
which one act of compassion has ramifications for everyone on the
planet, one act of cruelty touches us all. Such awareness, O'Hare told
his students, might enable them to attend more to being peace—not
just to waging peace or to making peace. To 'being peace.'[2]

Drawing on the thought of the Buddhist monk Thich Nhat Hahn,
O'Hare told the students Desert Storm was like a sheet of paper.
Quoting Nhat Hahn, he reminded them:

> If you are a poet, you will see clearly that there is a cloud float-
> ing in this sheet of paper. Without a cloud, there will be no rain;
> without rain, the trees cannot grow; and without trees, we cannot
> make paper. The cloud is essential for the paper to exist.

If we look into this sheet of paper even more deeply, we can see the sunshine in it. Without sunshine, the forest cannot grow. And so, we know that the sunshine is also in this sheet of paper....And if we continue to look, we see the logger who cut the tree and brought it to the mill to be transformed into paper. And we will see wheat. The logger cannot exist without his daily bread, and therefore the wheat that became his bread is also in this sheet of paper. The logger's father and mother are in it too.[3]

Then O'Hare made the connection. On that cold and frightening January morning, he told his students, "We are all in Operation Desert Storm."

* * *

In this essay, I want to suggest a catechesis directed to being peace. The title of my essay gives part of the game away: The particular form of the catechesis is born from the biblical Jubilee. But perhaps less obviously, the title is a reminder that in today's world, catechesis must draw not only on Christian resources, but on others beyond our own religious tradition. Although catechesis is a Christian term, describing the church educating through ministries such as liturgy, instruction, community, and works that serve justice, a catechesis toward "being peace" needs all the help it can get.

Thus my hope is to weave together the Buddhist theme of being peace, the Jewish theme of Jubilee, and the Catholic work of peace catechesis espoused by Pax Christi. In this interweaving, I draw comfort from the Vatican II document *Ad Gentes*, which reads, "Christians must learn to assimilate the ascetical and contemplative traditions planted by God in ancient cultures prior to the preaching of the Gospel" (paragraph 18). But I am comforted even more by the power that lies in realizing that being peace is the work of all of us together: Jewish, Christian, Buddhist, yes, but Muslim and Hindu and all other peoples too. Just as we were all in Desert Storm, we are all in the vocation of being peace.

Texts for the Catechesis

Three Scripture texts initiate the catechesis: one from the New Testament, the other two from the Hebrew Bible. The New Testament text is Luke 4:16-20. There, Jesus returns to Nazareth, where he was brought up, and goes to the synagogue on the sabbath, "as was his custom." When the time comes, he unrolls the scroll of the prophet Isaiah and finds the place where it was written:

The Spirit of God is upon me,

because God has anointed me

to bring good news to the poor.

God has sent me to proclaim release to the captives

and recovery of sight to the blind

to let the oppressed go free

to proclaim the year of God's favor.

Then he rolls up the scroll, gives it back to the attendant, and sits down. With the eyes of everyone in the synagogue fixed on him, he makes the stunning proclamation, "Today, this Scripture has been fulfilled in your hearing."

The second text is the reading from Isaiah chosen by Jesus on that sabbath, found in Isaiah 61, verses 1 and 2, and ending with the same phrase, "to proclaim the year of God's favor," leaving out—as

Luke records Jesus doing—the words that complete verse 2: "and the day of vengeance of our God, to comfort all who mourn."

The third text, however, is the centerpiece of the catechesis. This text is from the 25th chapter of the Book of Leviticus, and describes the Jubilee, "the year of God's favor," to which both Jesus and Isaiah pointed. They knew of the continuing ideal of the Jubilee in Jewish lore from their own Jewish roots and from centuries of Hebrew study of Torah. They knew it, too, from the practice of the sabbatical year, when the Jews regularly rested the land. They had learned Jubilee was a heightened, kairos time and an ideal that began with God saying to Moses on Mount Sinai, "Speak to the people of Israel and say to them, 'When you enter the land that I am giving you, the land shall observe a sabbath for God,'" and continued:

> Six years you shall sow your field, and six years you shall prune your vineyard and gather in their yield; but in the seventh year there shall be a sabbath of complete rest for the land, a sabbath for God: you shall not reap the aftergrowth of your harvest or gather the grapes of your unpruned vine: it shall be a year of complete rest for the land (verses 3-5).

Then, after those initial verses, the Jubilee proper was introduced.

> You shall count off seven weeks of years, seven times seven years, so that the period of seven weeks of years gives forty-nine years. Then you shall have the trumpet sounded loud; on the tenth day of the seventh month—on the day of atonement—you shall have the trumpet sounded throughout all your land. And you shall hallow the fiftieth year and you shall proclaim liberty throughout the land to all its inhabitants. It shall be a jubilee for you; you shall return, every one of you, to your property and every one of you to your family (verses 8-11).[4]

Scholars such as John Howard Yoder, Sharon Ringe, and André Trocmé tell us that both Jesus and Isaiah were referring to the year of Jubilee when they named the "year of God's favor."[5] Jesus and Isaiah knew Jubilee as a pattern and a plan that could serve as a complete religious grounding, a spirituality. Even more specifically, Yoder cites the Jubilee as a social ethic of nonviolence, which in its main themes turns human beings away from war, violence and vengeance, and directs our steps into the way of peace.[6]

The Jubilee does this by focusing on five major activities, each an element in our catechesis, each necessary as a completion of the others. Repeatedly addressed throughout the 55 verses of the entire 25th chapter of Leviticus, these are: (1) let the land lie fallow; (2) forgive all debts, granting remission of them; (3) release prisoners and those who are captives; (4) find out what belongs to whom and give it back (in today's economic terms, redistribute capital); and (5) sound the trumpet, celebrate, hold a great feast. In the catechesis that follows, I shall offer a brief description of each, and make some tentative suggestions how to embody them as elements in a "way" directed to being peace.

Let the Land Lie Fallow

As we begin the 21st century, the more sophisticated and the city folks among us finally know in our bones something that the less cluttered people never forgot: The land is our Mother, yes, and the land is our Sister. But most of all the land is our Home. Earth holds in its body our personal stories and those of our ancestors, making the land a "storied place." Earth keeps us alive, offering us air to breathe, water to drink. Earth receives us when we are born, and back into herself when we die. She is our primal ground.

Although we are her people, we have only recently become aware on a global scale how badly we've treated this

mother/sister/home. The biblical command once translated as "sub-
due" and "dominate" the earth has re-emerged as a command to
"befriend" and "dress" her, to walk tenderly as we cross her valleys
and plains, to stop in awe before her mountains and her sky.

Put another way, at this time in history we are once more honor-
ing the Jubilee command to let the land lie fallow. We modern earth
dwellers may think we discovered a spirituality assuming the intercon-
nectedness of land, water, air, non-human animals, but we didn't.
Instead, we find it sedimented in the words of a people three thousand
years ago: The land must be loved and rested in a measured,
solemn way.

That kind of care, leading us to tend to the earth outside us, is
intimately related to how we tend the land we ourselves are, how we
care for the earthly creation that is us, especially our bodies. The point
is that if we do this, we will be able to listen to and hear not only our
own deepest longings for peace, but those of all the earth's peoples.
We can do that by becoming people of receptivity who, taking time to
sit still, practice the art of inner peace, perhaps by repeating such
mantras as that found in T.S. Eliot's poetry: "Teach us to care and not
to care; teach us to sit still."

Nhat Hahn illuminates this element in catechesis. "Many people
are aware of the world's suffering, their hearts are filled with compassion," he writes. "They know what needs to be done, and they engage
in political, social and environmental work to try to change things."
But then he comments that after a period of intense involvement, they
find they lack the strength to sustain it any more. This is because that
strength arises from "deep inner peace."[7]

Let the land lie fallow. Unless we are willing to be still, to be
present to the world in the way the Sabbath of Jubilee teaches, we will

be unable to be peace to it. The irony of allowing the land to lie fallow is that precisely in this non-active activity, this not-doing, liberation is born and connections are made. Perhaps Pascal is still right: "All the world's troubles come from the inability to sit still in a room."

Catechetically, this will mean we attend to practices of stillness, quiet, and contemplative being. It may even develop into our never beginning nor ending a catechetical session without time to attend to our breath, repeating such words as "Breathing in, I am inhaling peace; breathing out, I am becoming peace" over and over. Such personal and individual breath mingles with the breath of others around the planet, and eventually joins the Holy Spirit, who continues to brood over the bent world with her own warm breath, and with her "ah! bright wings."[8]

The Forgiveness and Remission of Debts

Prayer leads us into the second component of Jubilee, which is directly related to Jesus' teaching concerning prayer. Jesus' Prayer, which is a highlight of this second Jubilee element, includes the request, "Forgive—remit—us our debts as we ourselves have also remitted them to our debtors." John Howard Yoder points out that the numerous versions translated as, "Forgive us our offenses as we forgive those who have offended us," are in error. Says Yoder,

> Accurately, the word *opheilema* of the Greek text signifies precisely a monetary debt, in the most material sense of the term. In the "Our Father," then, Jesus is not simply recommending vaguely that we might pardon those who have bothered us or made us trouble, but tells us purely and simply to erase the debts of those who owe us money; which is to say, practice the jubilee.[9]

For Yoder, moreover, Jesus' prayer "is genuinely a jubilary prayer."

The practice of forgiving debts was known to small kingdoms in the ancient Middle East; it was customary for rulers to grant general amnesties and cancel outstanding debts at the same time.[10] When the Jubilee teaching was formulated in ancient Israel, it drew on this tradition, but pointed to the God of Israel, not earthly rulers, as the source of amnesty and forgiveness. In a Jubilee year, employers were to cancel the debts of persons who didn't have the money to buy redemption from servitude, even as in their more personal one-on-one dealings, neighbors were to cancel each other's debts. The rationale for this remission was clear. The one doing the forgiving, letting go, cancelling debts must never forget, as the Bible puts it, "you were once strangers and sojourners; once upon a time your God redeemed you from the land of Egypt." All is gift. All belongs, ultimately, to the Divine Giver. Whatever we hold as our own must be grasped lightly.

For many of us, holding everything as gift is literally unthinkable. We spend much of our lives gathering possessions, and in worst-case scenarios, become what we have rather than what we are. Detachment, or divesting ourselves of possessions, doesn't appear on our life-screens. Yet strikingly, the ideal lives today, most noticeably among the poorest peoples of our world, especially those burdened by excruciating debt. As recently as 1991, missionaries who serve Panama's indigenous, African-descent and poor peasant communities demanded the World Bank and the United States pardon Latin America's crushing international debt and declare 1992 a year of Jubilee.[11] As an element in a catechesis for being peace, cancelling debt is a way to redress imbalances between those able to accumulate riches and those impoverished by the circumstance of being born poor, especially in so-called "debtor" nations.

On a personal level, this command also has profound consequences. If we are unable to cancel debts, to let go, and more generally to forgive, we are flawed as human beings. The inability becomes a knot, a stone in our psychic system, binding us from within. In contrast, the willingness to cancel monetary debts can release us as well as our debtors, can free us, bring us peace. It can enable us to let go of deeper, non-money debts: the hatreds and grudges stored up over decades that too often corrupt us and our relationships.

This often becomes easier as people age, or when health issues begin to trouble us and we recognize the essential giftedness of our physical selves: Simply being able to see, or to hear, to walk or to drive a car is a blessing. When death claims our parents, our most beloved companions, our spouses, even our children, we are reminded they too have been given, lent to us—as is everything—only for a time.

As part of catechesis, this teaching might be incarnated in particular practices of economic inventory, tithing and thanksgiving. Ideally, families and communities ought to keep open books, and regularly examine which debts need to be remitted. Tithing ought to include dipping into our principal as well as any extra funds we have, in memory of the widow Jesus commended as giving from her poverty, rather than from her overflow. For parishes and families, it will include bonding—twinning—with other communities in greater need than ourselves. But none of this ought to be separated from the other face of the coin: thanksgiving. Whenever we pause for Eucharist (which of course means thanksgiving), either the ritual meal of the assembled community or the daily Eucharists forming our family thanksgivings, expressing gratitude can be reminder and embodiment of the giftedness blessing us at every moment, even as it provides opportunity to lay down the heavy burden of uncollected debt.

Release the Prisoners

The Jubilee amnesty toward monetary debts extends to human beings too. When we cross the threshold into the special time of Jubilee and into the land God is giving us, even as God once gave Canaan to the Israelites, we are to work toward releasing today's indentured servants, bound by law or contract, as well as today's foreign detainees. Practicing hospitality, we are to give special care to strangers too, who may feel like prisoners in a foreign land. "If any who are dependent on you become so impoverished that they sell themselves to you, you shall not make them serve as slaves. In the year of Jubilee they and their children shall be free from your authority; they shall go back to their own family and return to their ancestral property" (verses 39-41).

Tragically, this is the most flawed element in the biblical Jubilee text, not for what it counsels, but for what it omits. For in addition to instruction that slides over the assumption that women were possessions, the text was written at a time when its freedom did not extend to enslaved people. Indentured servants, yes; strangers and detainees, yes; one's own family, yes. But the biblical writers did not yet see the humanity of those who had once been their wartime enemies-become-bounty property. Apparently, it did not occur to them to extend freedom to outside-the-family humans or former military enemies-become-possessions to be handed down from generation to generation. (See verses 44-46, a good place for catechists to pause and probe modern parallels).

Contemporary renderings of this part of the Jubilee text have corrected this oversight, this blind spot, so that the teaching and practice of Jubilee today extends to enslaved persons, an example of how the Bible corrects itself out of its own principles. Still, we may be tempted to stand back from these verses horrified, asking, "How could they have been so oblivious? How could they have failed to recognize that slaves were people—even more, as human beings, slaves were brothers and sisters?"

Tempting, until we turn the questions of freedom and release back on ourselves.

For this essential element in Jubilee challenges us—as persons, as communities, as nations—to examine our own omissions and to recognize what we gloss over; to study our own national histories of slavery. In those histories, some of our ancestors held humans as property and—as with child labor and child prostitution—still do. For others of us, it was our parents, our children, ourselves who were enslaved.

We can start this assessment in many places, but we dare not overlook our own prisons, where as chaplain and prisoner advocate Elaine Roulet notes, "a rich boy's prank is a poor boy's felony," and where incarceration takes an unfair toll on the families of the poorest in our midst. A nation's prisons reveal hidden, shadow sides of itself and make manifest the experiences of sisters and brothers the nation is reluctant to acknowledge. We are remarkably ignorant of women's prisons, for example, and the toll these take on mothers and children. Such prisons, too often, are places of warehousing, neither rehabilitating nor offering new beginnings.

Gretchen Wolff Pritchard, minister of Christian nurture at St. Paul's Episcopal Church in New Haven, has written and published a children's illustrated lectionary for over ten years. Last Advent, when the Isaiah 61 text was the week's Word, she included in her lectionary an image of a barred door flung open, with a ragged and emaciated figure leaping through it into the sunlight, with uplifted hands and a joyous face. When the picture appeared, she received a letter from a parent that read, in part,

> I don't feel the average kid reading this will come away with the idea of "set at liberty those who are oppressed." My eight-year-

old son's interpretation was more like "open up the jails and let everybody go." I'm not so sure Charles Manson and Ted Bundy fall into the oppressed category.

Commenting on that letter, Pritchard said the father didn't make it clear whether the child thought opening up the prisons and freeing everyone was bad news or good. But she did point out that the nightmare of murderers let loose (whether that was the parent's or the child's nightmare wasn't clear) was based on historical misunderstanding. For in the Bible, prisoners are not criminals or convicts, "since incarceration was not the penalty for civilian criminal acts. Rather they were prisoners of war, captives, hostages, victims of militarism or government oppression." Pritchard concluded by suggesting that children, more attuned to the imaginative world than many adults, tend to grasp this intuitively, and identify prisoners "as innocent good guys unjustly held, awaiting rescue by friends who are saying, 'We've got to save them!'"[12]

Pritchard's comment provides an opportunity to consider the connections between freeing prisoners and being peace, especially in a world where, as Amnesty International continues to document, imprisonment is a direct result of war or protest against war. But Pritchard also provokes us to turn inward to our own jailers. Jubilee's command to release prisoners points us inward as well as outward, prompting us to bring to light our own chains, our own slaveries, the cells we build in our souls. It alerts us to our addictions to money, drugs, youth. It assists us in discovering where our own unfreedoms intersect with our world's. It sobers us into a catechesis that includes asking, "What are my freedoms for?"

Find Out What Belongs to Whom and Give it Back

One of the common, indeed natural, impulses in mature adult life is giving back, paying back. As many people articulate this impulse, "I've been given so much; now it's my turn to give back, to return something of what I've received to others." This comment, which I suspect most of us have heard from friends and family, and probably said ourselves, is a way of witnessing to the gifts of life on one hand, and of giving thanks on the other.

Here I want to ground these impulses in the fourth essential component of Jubilee: find out what belongs to whom and give it back (the phrase is Walter Brueggemann's).[13] Grace is always being offered each of us to let go of the security of our present existence in order to search for the original Eden that is also our ultimate Home. That is the place Judy Chicago describes as where "All that has divided us will merge/Compassion will be wedded to power/And then everywhere will be called Eden once again."[14]

What is this fourth Jubilee element about? It is about justice.

In any complete catechesis toward being peace, justice is never far from the center. As the title of this book makes clear, we seek a "just peace." But a catechesis in this direction is not about a blindfold-ed figure weighing scales evenly. Instead, the concern of biblical and religious justice is restoring broken, shattered relations to harmony and balance. Justice has to do with creating conditions enabling things and people to be themselves.

The land is just if it is able to produce grain and the fruits of the earth; the water is just if it can sustain life; the tree is just if it can stand and grow towards the sky, unafraid of air pollution or a silent spring. A cat is just if it can stretch and sleep and stretch again; a kangaroo if it can leap. And human beings are just when we live our responsibility to stand humbly, listening to our universe, and doing what we can to make justice happen. For humans, being just means being faithful to the demands of all our relationships.[15]

The key to this work lies in Jubilee: finding out what belongs to whom and giving it back. Proclaiming liberty to all the inhabitants of the universe by letting them be what they are. "The land shall not be sold in perpetuity," says our God, "for the land is mine." But in the meantime, at no more than fifty-year intervals, the land shall be returned to its original owners.

It is hard to imagine what this might mean for relations between the U.S. and Mexico, for example, concerning places such as Texas. And, as Sarah Epperly writes, "It is difficult to imagine a legal means of restoring the land to the Native Americans. The land may be re-titled to a particular tribe, and this does happen, but the way of life that the tribe knew can't be 'lived out' on the land and in the society in which the tribe now finds itself." Yet, she goes on,

> It does seem to me that this society might begin to live in such a manner that the reverence for life that the Native American has for the earth, water, sky, vegetation, etc. might re-emerge. We might begin on a personal level by eating only the amounts of food required for a healthful life so that we "want not" but also "waste not." Other examples:

> (a) use laundry detergents that do not pollute the streams;

> (b) rainbow trout fishing in Alaska, in which rainbow are sport-fished, but with special barbless hooks; anglers are taught how to hold fish to remove the hook, then the fish is gently returned to the water and set free;

(c) white-water rafting expeditions that must leave the water and shoreline as it was; even the ashes from the campfire carried off.[16]

Still, the bottom line of this aspect of Jubilee is the redistribution of capital. As United States citizens, this means we lobby for and take part in the work, already begun (such as in Haiti, Central America, South Africa) of restoring independence to nations or peoples under the domain of others, assisting the return to them of the capital that is land. It means pursuing theologies of relinquishment. It means easing, and in many cases protesting, the paying and overpaying of exorbitant interest rates by other countries towards our own.

This is probably the aspect of Jubilee that sticks most in the throats of contemporary capitalists. To return to the fourth chapter of Luke's Gospel, where having listened to Jesus' declaration of Jubilee, the people began to realize what he was urging on them, this can be a hard, hard saying. Finally understanding what Jesus was getting at, and frightened it would mean giving up too much, those Nazarenes began muttering the Aramaic equivalent of "Who does he think he is?" As the ramifications of his words became clear, they "filled with rage. They got up, drove him out of the town, and led him to the brow of the hill on which their town was built, so that they might hurl him off the cliff. But he passed through the midst of them and went on his way (verses 28-30)."

That can be a reaction to those of us who urge similar justice today. But it is also possible that today we may finally be ready to live out this Jubilee command, due to the awareness born from global inter-communication. "Such a redistribution of capital, accomplished every fifty years by faithfulness to the righteous will of God and in the expectation of the kingdom, would today be nothing utopian," concludes John Howard Yoder. Instead, "many bloody revolutions would have been avoided if the Christian church had shown herself more respectful than Israel was of the jubilee dispositions contained in the law of Moses."[17] To redistribute capital, then, could become a pathway into insuring a global people schooled to the vocation of being peace.

Hold a Great Feast

Whenever I lead a retreat on Jubilee, or teach or catechize on the theme, someone with a theology background invariably asks me, "Why has Jubilee never been tried?" The questioner knows that despite its recurrence as an ideal throughout human history, despite serious pleas from economists, prisoners, or debtor nations, Jubilee has yet to be lived, yet to be practiced in all its fullness.

My own hunch why that's never happened is that it's due to an incomplete catechesis. Somewhere along the line, we've learned a too narrow meaning for Jubilee. We think of it as equivalent to feasting and give our attention solely to festivity and celebration. This can be a particular danger if we are Catholic Christians, very practiced in throwing many, many parties.

This doesn't translate as "forego feasting," for if we did, the stones would cry out. Our God is not grim. Jesus' first miracle was providing more wine at a wedding celebration, and Jubilee and the God of Jubilee command us to feast. But we can't feast completely unless we also let the land lie fallow, remit debts, free prisoners, and return what belongs to others. Every aspect of Jubilee is connected to every other. Touch one and the rest quiver. We acknowledge such interconnection whenever we offer a grace like this one before a meal: "Thank you for this food. To those who hunger, grant bread. To those with bread, grant hunger for justice." In such a prayer, we rejoice in bread and in a meal if we're lucky enough to have food; we also ritually recognize our human responsibility to those who don't.

That said, we now attend to the last Jubilee command: "Stop everything. Sound the trumpet, the yobel (which gives us the word Jubilee).[18] Celebrate. Sing the song of liberation everywhere. It's time to proclaim the year of God's favor. It's time for Jubilee."

Many biblical commentators associate this command with John the Baptist and with Jesus of Nazareth and the beginnings of Christianity. When John and Jesus said, "The Kingdom of God is at hand; repent; believe the Good News, for now is the time of salvation," they didn't do so pretentiously or pompously. Instead, they joyfully and delightedly proclaimed a Jubilee Time, an enduring celebration ushering in a new era, another kind of century, a millennium of just peace.

Yoder points out that most people know "kingdom" is a political term. But, he says, the ordinary religious woman or man is less aware that "Gospel," good news, is also political. It refers not to any old welcome report, any old good news, but to the kind of important proclamation worth sending a runner, worth sounding the trumpet, worth holding a public feast when the runner arrives.[19]

So too the news of Jubilee. So too the end of the century. So too the beginning of a new millennium in the 21st century. We have already begun this renewed Jubilee time as a time to let the land lie fallow, cancel debts, unlock prison doors. We have begun the possibility of a great feast, as we attempt to find out what belongs to others and give that back. We are discovering a strength coming from the knowledge of rich resources on which we may draw, not only in our own, but in other religious traditions. Through the gift of Jubilee, and as no other people or time in history, perhaps, we hold in our hands and minds and hearts the possibility of being peace.

Maria Harris is a Catholic religious educator who has taught at New York University, John Carroll University, Andover Newton Theological School and Auburn Theological Seminary. She has published eighty-five articles and thirteen books, including Dance of the Spirit, Jubilee Time *and* Proclaim Jubilee!.

Notes:

1. Padraic O'Hare, in *Alternative Newsletter* 17, 3 (February, 1991), pp. 2-3. See also his *The Way of Faithfulness: Contemplation and Formation in the Church* (Valley Forge, Pennsylvania: Trinity Press International, 1993) for extensive use of Buddhist tradition in the education of Catholic Christians.

2. Thich Nhat Hahn, *Being Peace* (Berkeley: Parallax Press, 1987). The phrase "being peace" is like a mantra, whose meaning continues revealing itself as we dwell with it. It teaches us that if we court vengeance, we become vengeance; if we court love we become love; if we court peace, we become peace.

3. Thich Nhat Hahn, *Peace Is Every Step* (New York: Bantam Books, 1992), p. 95.

4. All Scripture quotes are from the New Revised Standard Version (New York: Oxford University Press, 1989).

5. See John Howard Yoder, *The Politics of Jesus* (Grand Rapids: Eerdmans, 1972); Sharon Ringe, *Jesus, Liberation and the Biblical Jubilee* (Philadelphia: Fortress, 1985); and André Trocmé, *Jesus-Christ et la revolution non-violente* (Geneva: Labor and Fides, 1961), on which Yoder draws.

6. See Yoder, *The Politics of Jesus*; see also Stanley Hauerwas, "When the Politics of Jesus Makes a Difference," in *Christian Century* (October 13, 1993), pp. 982-987.

7. Nhat Hahn, *Peace Is Every Step*, p. 99.

8. In "God's Grandeur," Gerard Manley Hopkins writes that "...the Holy Ghost over the bent/World broods with warm breast and with ah! bright wings." See *A Hopkins Reader*, edited by John Pick (Garden City: Doubleday, 1966), pp. 47-48.

9. Yoder, p. 66.

10. See Ringe, pp. 22-25.

11. See *National Catholic Reporter* (February, 1991), p. 8. Eventually such petitions grew into movements such as Jubilee 2000.

12. In "Living by the Word: Good News" in *Christian Century* (December 1, 1993), p. 1203.

13. See Walter Brueggemann in *To Act Justly, Live Tenderly, Walk Humbly* (New Jersey: Paulist, 1986), pp. 5-28.

14. From *The Dinner Party* (Garden City: Doubleday, 1979), p. 256.

15. Much of this meaning of justice is from John Donahue, "Biblical Perspectives on Justice," in *The Faith That Does Justice*, edited by John C. Haughey (New York: Paulist, 1977), pp. 69 ff.

16. Sarah Epperly's comments are in a private communication to me.

17. Yoder, pp. 76-77.

18. On meanings of yobel, see Ringe, pp. 25-28.

19. Yoder, p. 34.

THE FALL OF BABEL: O HAPPY FAULT!

By Rosemary Luling Haughton

Once upon a time, everyone spoke the same language, says the story. So everyone understood what everyone else was saying. Since there was nobody to say, "what does that mean?" it seemed to those people that they knew all there was to know. This gave them a great feeling of confidence and power. After all, there was nothing they couldn't explain, no ambiguities, no doubts. (They didn't even have a word for "doubt," because doubt can only occur when someone outside a system questions something within it. If there is no "outside," the system appears to be perfect and all-encompassing.)

In spite of this happy conviction, something was causing anxiety. Nobody mentioned it because nobody could identify it, and there were no words for it. But for some reason, the mere fact of being one people with one language didn't seem quite enough. So some people came up with the idea of building a city and a tower, because the city would express the oneness and completeness of the perfect culture, and the tower, by its strength and height, would express the greatness of a united people. (But I don't suppose they had a word for "united," because they couldn't envisage anything else.)

By building the city and tower, they would do two things: They would make sure that, whatever form of government they had, it could easily control the population, and they would include God in their culture. After all, they had a word for God, and a word for heaven, and it was only right, in that case, to make it clear that God (in heaven) was one of themselves. Heaven should be reached by their tower, as it was reached by their language.

When God noticed what was going on, says the story, God was

very upset. "If they do this, nothing will be beyond them," God said. This sounds as if God felt threatened by the united people and their high tower, but on closer examination, it seems possible that there was another explanation for this account of how God reacted. After all, we have only their story of how God felt, and they had their own reasons for creating this particular explanation, as we shall see.

For what happened next was very humiliating. Suddenly, people found they couldn't understand one another. A master mason opened his mouth to tell a journeyman where to lay the next course of bricks for the tower, and the journeyman made a sign against the evil eye, because the order sounded like a magic spell. Husbands gave orders to wives and the wives rushed for the doctor, convinced the men were feverish; teachers began a lesson, and the children screamed with laughter and ran off to play; when government officials made speeches, their underlings sent for the ambulance (or whatever equipment they had in those days).

But soon the people stopped laughing and began to be very afraid. They stopped building, too, because no one could read the plans or give or take orders. They couldn't trade, or teach, or rule, or even grow crops, because they couldn't make decisions together about anything. They faced starvation.

Then the first panic died down a little. People stopped running around and screaming with rage and were just walking around, staring at one another in bewilderment, desperately trying out a few words here and there. To their relief, they then discovered that some people did understand one another.

Soon, those who understood one another began to gather together, feeling as if at last they had found a few sane people among a mob of lunatics. But it was clear to those who did understand one another that they couldn't live together with the lunatics in the half-built city, let alone finish the tower. There weren't enough in any one group that spoke the same language, and besides, you never knew what the lunatics might choose to do. So, although the language groups couldn't communicate from group to group or plan, each group began to do the same thing: to collect a few possessions and leave, putting as much distance as possible between themselves and all the other groups.

Since there was plenty of space, each group found an area where it could settle without any contact with any other group. They all settled down and built towns and cities and grew crops and raised children, and they found (to their relief) that the children spoke the same language as their parents.

But as the years passed, those children grew up and began to ask questions. "What happened to my grandfather, if he isn't buried here?" "There are pieces of furniture and jewelry here quite different from those we make now, and older. Where did they come from?" And— worst of all—they asked, "Are there other people, beyond the mountains, or through the forests, or beyond the plains, or are we the only ones?"

Those who remembered the long-ago trek to a new country had their reply. Once, they said, we were one very great people, and we understood one another, and we knew we were so great that we could do anything. We even began to build a tower high enough to reach to heaven, so that we could talk to God. But God was jealous of our greatness. God wanted to be sure God was still greater. So God cast a spell on most of the people, so that they went mad and could only talk nonsense. We had to leave; it was too dangerous to stay there. We believe those crazy people are living somewhere, but we have nothing to do with them. They aren't like us. After all, we are the ones who have the one real language, and even if God deprived us of our power, we are the only ones who understand God.

This kind of conversation was going on among each of the groups scattered by their inability to understand one another. Of course, each group told the story a little differently, but they all took it for granted that they were the ones who spoke the real language, and that all the rest were crazy—or maybe just backward, since it must have taken them a long time to discover a way to communicate, poor things.

So the generations passed and the populations grew, and after a time, the different groups spread out so far that they realized, with a shock, that others, not of their language group, were living not so far away. When they got used to the idea, some people would travel to the settlements of another group, out of curiosity, to see what went on. All of them came home with stories of people who built very peculiar houses, wore the most outrageous clothes, (or—worse still—hardly any clothes!) and, of course, talked a language that made no sense.

As long as they visited each other only out of curiosity, no harm was done. Even if they were not always quite polite to each other, they tended to behave reasonably well, because the visitors were heavily outnumbered. But as populations grew, some groups began to realize that another group had very fertile land, or forests with excellent timber, or that they used tools that showed they had mineral deposits, and altogether that they were better off than their neighbors who were running out of fertile land, or lumber, and lacked mineral resources.

It seemed to the groups who needed these commodities that it was unnatural to leave them in the possession of people who, after all, were only barely emerged from lunacy—not "real" people at all. The next step was to consider how to obtain these resources. The usual way, if the "real" people were numerous enough, was to kill off the possessors and take over their land. Since those who were killed were not real people, it was just like ridding yourself of dangerous wild animals.

But there were some who, observing the people who were "backward," did not approve of the killing. They had spent some time among people of another group and felt that they were possibly quite intelligent, and certainly capable of learning. They could be trained to provide goods and services for the "real" people. This would be good for them, since they would then learn to speak "real" language and wear "real" clothes and eat "real" food and even be taught about the "real" God. But first, of course, they must be subdued and made to obey.

So it went on: The stronger language groups (meaning those who could develop the best weapons) seized the lands of weaker ones and made those people work for their conquerors, or else killed them. Some of these "weaker" groups, seeing what went on, escaped into remote forests and mountains and maintained their own language, protected by distance and by lack of interest. Nobody really wanted what they had. (But they, too, believed that they were the real people and—perhaps excusably—that those who had driven them away were not real people but evil demons.) So fighting and conquering and re-conquering, or avoiding conquest or subverting it, became the normal way for groups to interact.

It is true that one of the most powerful groups included people who became very concerned about all the killing, because they had developed a story about God that proclaimed peace as God's will. Although most of them agreed that, in practice, war was unavoidable, they tried to mitigate its horrors by laying down some rules about war. They demanded that warring factions should have a good reason for killing and should only kill those who themselves took up arms. In practice, none of this made any difference, but it provided a subject for a lot of books.

So there it was: a world populated by people who all spoke different languages, and dressed differently and ate differently and built differently and organized themselves differently, and believed different things about God. Each group believed that it spoke the only real language and lived in the only sensible way and worshipped the only true God. But some groups that were strong recognized that they couldn't conquer other strong groups. If they tried, they would get killed themselves. Though they might despise one another, they still wanted things that other strong groups grew or made. So, instead of trying to seize them by force, they bargained for them; they exchanged value for value. How do you do that if you don't speak the other's language? Well, like it or not, once you have reached the limits of sign language, you learn to speak it. So, little by little, it became clear that speaking another language (however debased) could be a way to prosper.

It was a very long time before the descendants of the refugees from the city and the tower began to admit to themselves that other languages made as much sense as their own, and even to explore the homelands of other groups with pleasure, and open restaurants selling foreign food. Even then, the strongest groups of all, while admitting the beauty and antiquity of other languages and ways, still believed that, for really successful living, there was only one language and one way—their own. That meant that, ideally, others should be forced to do things the way the "real" people did, for their own good, of course. The idea that there was only one real language died hard.

But in the end, when great powers had come near to annihilating themselves and all others, and in the process impoverished and displaced huge populations and spread disease and devastation, and while smaller ones were still killing each other, and impoverishing each other, a few people from many different groups came together and began to talk about why all this killing and near killing, this devastation and misery, had ever begun.

This coming together was possible because, just to survive and compete, people now knew a lot about other people. They even knew the different versions of the story of the tower and the city that were told by different groups. Those who began to meet together could not only speak one another's languages, but they knew one another's stories well enough to discuss certain similarities as well as differences. But they felt that, even if all those stories could be reconciled, there was still something wrong—or else why all this misery and hate? Surely, people weren't meant to live like that. And if people felt that God meant them to be like that, then they must have the wrong idea about God.

In the end, these strange people came to the conclusion that there was something wrong with the story of the city and the tower as they had been told it. In particular, there was something wrong with the part about God: If God had really condemned all those people, and their descendants, to be unable to communicate and therefore to hate and exploit and kill each other, then this God was very evil. But they knew that growth and abundance and joy and courage and beauty and love were gifts of God and showed God's nature. The old story didn't fit the God they had come to know—all of them in different ways. Definitely, something was wrong.

One day, as these unusual people were puzzling over this discrepancy, one person spoke up—rather softly, because it sounded outrageous.

"Suppose God did not make our ancestors mad, or drive them away from the city in so many directions, because God was afraid of them and wanted to punish them, but because God loved them? Maybe God knew it was better for people to be different. Maybe God saw that trying to be all the same, and knowing everything, was not good for us."

There was a long hush, broken only by a few shocked cries of "oh" and "oh, no" and "ah!" Then another person, still very softly, said: "Then perhaps all this mess happened simply because we didn't want to understand what God was doing. We were too proud and self-righteous. We were still trying, in separate groups, to do what our ancestors tried to do when they built the tower."

"Now I understand!" said someone else, a bit more loudly. "You all remember how difficult it was for us to learn each other's languages, and all the different stories, but how learning all that gave us wonderful new insights. It made us understand our own language, our own stories, so much better. That's what God wanted. Being different wasn't meant to be a punishment, but an opportunity. God didn't break up our language out of fear, but out of love. But we didn't want to understand."

Then, of course, everyone began talking at once, louder and louder, and someone suggested that celebration was appropriate. So they all went home and came back later with the food and drink that each group liked best, and they had a wonderful party, because at last they understood the joy of being different. Each group danced the dances of their people, and sang the songs of their people, and all present wondered at the richness and joy that could be shared.

Of course, it wasn't enough for these few people to understand. When the party was over, they sat down and spent a long time planning how they might spread the message and convince everyone that being different was a gift from God, not a curse, that human beings needed to be different in order to achieve the fullness of which they are capable.

They knew it was going to be hard, because the habits of pride, of desire to dominate, of dislike and contempt for those of other languages and with other stories, were so well established, and also so important to a sense of group identity, that to let these things go could feel like suicide. But they had hope, because at last they could tell the stories of a God who could only be known in the mystery that lies between meanings, in the awesome wisdom that escapes all language but is encountered in the generous exchange of difference.

Perceiving this, they knew that war and competition made no sense, but they also recognized that peace was not something that must be precariously imposed on beings naturally violent and suspicious, who were to be tamed only by fear of sanctions. They understood more and more deeply that, on the contrary, peace is inherent, and justice prevails once people are freed from fear. For a long time, the rest of the world regarded these people as, at best, impractical mystics and, at worst, dangerous subversives. Indeed, many were killed or imprisoned, but they persevered, because they believed that in the end, greed, stupidity and self-deception become self-defeating, so that even the most willfully blind would come to recognize that the old ways did not work.

When that time comes, they told one another, although millions may be malnourished and diseased, the fertile earth ravaged and polluted, ancestral treasures lost forever, there will be (scattered across the earth, as their ancestors were scattered for a very different reason) little gatherings of people who have learned how to live in peace and how to heal the land and the people. Then the goal of all people will no longer be to reach the heavens, as if God could be controlled, but to know one another in all the richness of difference, and so to know the Spirit indwelling in all creatures, who can make all things new.

Rosemary Luling Haughton is one of a group who developed and is still involved in the Wellspring Home, in Gloucester, Mass. Wellspring Home is a community-based organization engaged in justice work, in particular, work with and for women in poverty, through education, family shelter, economic development and housing. Author of over thirty books, Haughton also lectures. Her lastest books are The Tower That Fell *and* Images For Change, *both from Paulist Press.*

Obedience and Vocation: Faithful Resistance

By Elizabeth McAlister

The trouble with our state
was not civil disobedience
which, in any case, was hesitant and rare.
Civil disobedience was rare as kidney stone
No, rarer; it was disappearing like immigrant's disease.
You've heard of a war on cancer?
There is no war like the plague of media
There is no war like routine
There is no war like three square meals
There is no war like the prevailing wind
It blows softly; whispers "don't rock the boat"!
the sails obey, the ship of state rolls on.
The trouble with our state—
we learned only afterward
when the dead resembled the living who resembled the dead
and civil virtue shone like paint on tin
and tin citizens and tin soldiers marched to the common whip
—our trouble
the trouble with our state
with our state of soul
our state of seige—
was
civil
obedience.   Daniel Berrigan, S.J.

Do people, "movement" people, believe their own rhetoric? Do I, as a "movement person," believe my own rhetoric? I was so struck by Bishop Thomas Gumbleton speaking in Seattle in November 1987, explaining his passage into resistance and civil disobedience—a passage animated, at least in part, by listening to what he himself had been saying for years? Do we believe our own rhetoric, speeches, leaflets? More: Do we act and live as if we believed them?

I get this question all the time: "How could you go to prison and leave your children?" Some question in a spirit of praise for a courage they presume I have and equally presume they don't have. Others ask in a spirit that is profoundly critical of my lack of responsibility and my lack of feeling for my children.

And I answer: "For the same reason I would put my body between my children and an armed raving maniac if could!" If my action seems heroic or irresponsible or unfeeling, it can only mean that there is a difference in my perception and that of my questioners. I believe my children—all our children—are in danger, are endangered. But my questioners don't. It's that simple. Or that complex.

Or I get this approach: "Well, this resistance—it's your vocation. Yours is the prophetic vocation, whereas mine is service, or ministry, or...." So I've wondered a lot about this business of vocation. What is the meaning of vocation in that context? And it feels to me as though it is something that people do well, that they like to do, that is their source of income, that maintains them in the lifestyle to which they have become accustomed.

What, by contrast, is the meaning of vocation biblically?

The concordance gives us but one reference to "vocation" in Scripture, in Ephesians 4:1. "As a prisoner for God, then, I urge you to live a life worthy of the calling [vocation] you have received." Then I looked up the term "calling" and found that it is a Pauline term more than a Gospel term. It is found nine times in Paul, once in Peter.[1]

"Called" is the term used for the call to the disciples. And, like so much of Scripture, it is in the imperative mood—a command, more than the gentle whisper suggested by vocation. And it is addressed to all!

If we read Mark 3:13-19, we see Jesus withdrawing from the fray and going up the mountain with handpicked followers. Those who "came and joined him" were particularly committed companions of Jesus.

Jesus' choice of a mountain setting is as provocative as it is premeditated. The site for divinely inspired activity—for conspiracy. A conspiracy is formed. The thirteen breathed together that fecund thinner air. None could descend quite the same person, though actual performance is still a long way from transformation. The mountaintop events are rather straightforwardly recorded by Mark. They are twofold: He named them and he called them.

Names bring one into the light. In this case, a new light. A wholly new kind of arrangement is being forged. One that will fly in the face of every systemically designed order, or so-called "order," such as the nuclear family, the institution, the nation-state. The malignancy of the social fabric will be rocked by such comings-together, such conspiracies, such bondings.

Twelve are named in this reading. The list is hardly an inclusive rendering of those who chose to be chosen. Seven are never mentioned again (by name, that is) in Mark's narrative. Numerous other close and faithful companions are not noted among the twelve, such as the Marys, Levi and Martha. Given that we know how this Jesus plot unfolds, a reading of some of the cast of characters is a bit distracting, especially with the passage's closing footnote on Judas. An ominous line. And, too, we know that all mentioned were most decidedly hard to find in a faithless way later on.

"Who are my kin?" Jesus said. "Those who hear the word of God and keep it." That is to say, those who keep it audible. Keep it alive. Keep it going. And us? Where do we fit in the never-ending plot? Are we faithful enough to be wanted? Wanting enough to be faithful?

"Calling," or "vocation," is a noun, a thing. (In a real way, it has become a possession). "Called" is what the disciples were on the mountain, what we are—that is, under orders. It is a verb, a verb of which we are the objects, rather than objects we hold. The difference makes all the difference. Our submission to being called changes everything. We are people on a mission; people whose fidelity to that mission gives life to them and to all whom they touch; people whose fidelity is the only source of hope that I know.

Obedience to the call of Christ will mean disobedience to the myriad calls of the culture. The problem is too little divine obedience, too few who accept their God-given name (Christian) and their status as called.

WANTED: Good News, which of course means laborers, those willing to spread Good News, "free-form men and women."

WANTED: Hope. Imagination. The stuff that allows for that which cannot, by definition, be seen.

WANTED: Virtuous power. A compassionate ordering. No more Salvadorans marked for death. Or Nicaraguans. Or Iranians. Or Russians. Or children.

WANTED: One hardy weed, springing through concrete.

WANTED: Persons willing to be at large. At home being at large. At home being wanted...

WANTED: Willing collaborators to today's conspiracy. The one that was kicked off in the margins, on a mountaintop so obscure as to not be named. The one that formally listed only 12 participants.

WANTED: Reconstructed swords, that is, plowshares and land for people to plow.

WANTED: Pruning hooks and orchards for people to prune.

WANTED: 24 hours, or thereabouts, to midnight.

WANTED: A Who's Who of those willing to say "Yes" to Power's "No."

WANTED: The faithful absurdity of Odysseus.[2]

The "wants" are not so mysterious, nor the means. And yet, why so hard to find?

The problem is too much civil obedience. And here is our bind, is it not? During most of human history, obedience has been identified with virtue, and disobedience with sin. This identification between disobedience and sin has a stranglehold on us all. And all too often it comes down to this: As long as I am obedient to the power of the state or the church, or public opinion, (and often the difference is no difference) I feel four things that are important to us as human beings:

I feel safe and protected.
My obedience makes me part of the power I worship, and so I feel strong.
I feel righteous, and I can make no error, since it decides for me.
I cannot be alone, because it watches over me.
In order to disobey, one must have the courage to be at risk, to be unsafe, to be weak, to be in error or sin, and to be alone.
Yet we know that our spiritual development depends on the presence of people who dare to say "No!" to the powers that be in the name of their conscience or their faith. And we know that

our intellectual development depends on the presence of people who dare to be disobedient to authorities who try to muzzle new thoughts, and to the authority of long-established opinions that declared change to be nonsense.

The question of disobedience is of vital importance today. According to the Bible, human history began with an act of disobedience by Adam and Eve. According to Greek myth, civilization began with Prometheus' act of disobedience. But it is not unlikely that human history will be terminated by an act of obedience—obedience to authorities who themselves are obedient to archaic fetishes of "state sovereignty" and "national honor" and "military victory." Those authorities will give the orders to push the fatal buttons to those who are obedient to them and to their fetishes.[3]

I say "archaic fetishes" because, while we are living technically in the Atomic Age, the majority of people, including most who are in power, live emotionally in the Stone Age. While our math, astronomy, and natural sciences are of the 21st century, most of our ideas about politics, the state, and society lag far behind the age of science. (A reiteration of Einstein: "The splitting of the atom has changed everything except our thinking, and so we drift to unparalleled disaster.")

If we commit suicide, it will be because people:

will obey those who command them to push the deadly buttons;

will obey the archaic passions of fear, hate and greed;

will obey obsolete clichés of state sovereignty-national honor.

That many good people "do good" but stop short of civil disobedience (as not "their thing") is not to be argued. In their doing good, they allow evil to flourish unabated, unmasked, even unquestioned. It is as if they do not have any grasp of the realities of the government under which we live. This was brought home to me at Maryknoll one summer not too long ago. Students in the peace and justice program there were having a great deal of difficulty with what Phil and I were saying about the biblical mandate to resistance. To them, it seemed judgmental toward all the good people they knew, doing good work for others. As student after student came back to this point, I suddenly had this image of hosts of good people who remain silent in the face of terrible evils—their silence allowing the evils to continue. And the image of what it would mean if they all joined together and shouted out against that evil. Suddenly I felt I understood Dan's poem. They are indeed the problem. The problem is civil obedience. Or as Dorothy Day said: "Our problems stem from our acceptance of this filthy, rotten system."

The mission from the mountain, you will remember, was to preach the good news and to cast out demons, to confront evil. But do we confront the evil? Or do we insulate ourselves against it by the "vocation" we choose for ourselves—the vocation that enables us to accept the name given to us by the culture, consumers, over the name given to us in Christ? "Homo consumens" is a human creation, not a divine creation—a being under the illusion of happiness, while suffering boredom and passivity. The more power we have over machines, the more powerless we become as human beings; the more we consume, the more we become slaves to the ever-increasing needs the industrial system creates and manipulates. We mistake thrill and excitement for joy and happiness, and material comfort for aliveness; satisfied greed becomes the meaning of life, the striving for it a new religion. The freedom to consume becomes the essence of human freedom.

How, in each of our lives, do we deal with that evil? I'm trying to figure this out. I'm trying to understand why resistance to our criminal government still appears strange or exceptional or heroic, even in the face of Nicaragua, El Salvador, Panama, the radical changes in the

Soviet Union, in Eastern Europe. I'm trying not to be judgmental. Maybe it helps to extrapolate like this. There is, is there not, this deep rift in our psyches/souls between what we think and what we do. We are split personalities. None of us is exempt from this. I can't think of any American who is not contributing in some way to destruction. To live undestructively would require a great deal more work than we've been able to do.

But some are more destructive. Some are more conscious of their destructiveness. For the former, it is a "practical" compromise, a necessary reality, the price of modern comfort and convenience. For the latter, it is an agenda for thought and work that may produce remedies. Once our personal connection to what is wrong becomes clear, then we have to choose: go on as before or begin the effort to change the way we think and live.

That will mean, at least in part, that we stand by what we say, that we believe it, that we become accountable for it, that we be willing to act on it. Fidelity to our word as given. Being faithful to our word as given, standing by it, believing it, acting on it, involves us in a different kind of future. It's as if, by our word, we make a promise, a promise that binds us to someone else's future—maybe to the future of humanity and our earth, if we believe our own leaflets.

If the promise is serious enough, we come to the making of it by love, and in awe and fear. Fear, love, awe bind us to no selfish purpose but to each other. And they force from us a kind of speaking that is at once more exact and more binding than common speech or the speech used to sell consumer goods. Because when we promise in love and awe and fear, we give up some of our mobility. We give up the ability to bob and weave with new twists and turns in the culture. We are speaking where we stand now in faith and we shall stand afterwards—

in the presence of what we have said—faithful! In hope!

Elizabeth McAlister is a long-time anti-war activist who lives at Jonah House in Balitmore. She is married to Phillip Berrigan and has three children.

Notes:

1. Romans 11:20; 1 Corinthians 1:26 and 7:20; Ephesians 1:18 and 4:4; Philippians 3:1; 2 Thessalonians 1:11; 2 Timothy 1:9; Hebrews 3.1; and 2 Peter 1:10.

2. Odysseus' is a journey home after 20 years of wandering. The Odyssey begins in the world of "The lliad," a world which, like our own, is war-obsessed, preoccupied with "manly" deeds of exploitation, anger, aggression, pillage, and the disorder, uprootedness and vagabondage that are their result. At the end of the poem, Odysseus moves away from the values of the world toward the values of peace. He was instructed by the ghost of the seer Teiresias to perform a ritual of atonement. Carrying an oar on his shoulder, he must walk inland until be comes to a place where people have no knowledge of the sea or ships, where a passerby will mistake his oar for a winnowing fan. There he must plant his oar in the ground and make a sacrifice to the sea god, Poseidon. Odysseus will not know rest until he has seen the symbol of his warrior life become a farming tool.

3. Erich Fromm's essay "Prophets and Priests" in *On Disobedience*, p.48).

Appendix

Modern War and Christian Conscience

This editorial appeared in La Civiltà Cattolica, *on July 6, 1991. This English text, published by* Origins, *a service of the National Conference of Catholic Bishops, is based on a translation by the Rev. William Shannon, professor emeritus of religious studies at Nazareth College in Rochester, New York.*

Only a few months have passed since the Gulf War, which began during the night of Jan. 16-17, 1991, and ended Feb. 28, 1991; and yet hardly anyone speaks about it. In fact, a heavy silence has fallen, as if people want to remove it from their consciences as quickly and as totally as possible. The most curious thing about it is that, while at other times and in similar circumstances people would rush to discover and report what really happened, we still to this day do not know what actually took place during the Gulf War.

We do not know, for example, the most essential data: How many Iraqis—military and civilian—lost their lives? Why hasn't this been made known by one side or the other? (Surely someone knows.) Was it perhaps because it was a huge and futile "massacre," and it was expedient—politically, though certainly not morally—that people remain uninformed?

In any case the war in the Gulf has most dramatically reawakened the Christian conscience—and, we believe, also the secular conscience—to the problem of modern warfare.

Why do we speak of "modern warfare" and not simply of "war"? Because modern warfare is radically different from wars of the past, and therefore the theoretical categories and moral judgments that applied to past wars no longer seem applicable to modern warfare.

133

True, war remains fundamentally the same: mortal combat, nourished by hatred, in which physical violence in all its brutality is let loose with the intention of "subduing" (K. von Clausewitz) or "destroying" (Mao Tse-tung) the enemy. In fact, Karl von Clausewitz writes:

> War is nothing other than a duel on a wider scale. Each one attempts with physical force to make the other submit to his will: The immediate intention is to overthrow the adversary so as to render him (sic) incapable of resistance. War, therefore, is an act of violence designed to force the adversary to do our will. Violence, in order to confront violence, arms itself with the inventions of the arts and sciences. It is accompanied by minimal restrictions, scarcely worth mentioning, which it prescribes in the name of international law but which in reality do not weaken its own power. Violence, that is physical violence,...is therefore the means; the end is to impose our will on the enemy. To reach this end without fail, it is necessary to disarm the enemy (Della Guerra, Rome, 1941, 19s).

War, in other words, is always an evil. But its wickedness becomes so much more evident when one looks at modern warfare. If wars of the past, because of the relatively limited losses involved, could be justified by some people as the lesser evil, this can no longer be said of modern warfare. How did we move from war to modern warfare? As Karl von Clausewitz remarks, war, with all the violence it implies, "arms itself with the inventions of the arts and sciences" and therefore changes little by little as weapons perfected by scientific inventions become more and more destructive and homicidal. For instance, the introduction of gunpowder caused the first great revolution in the art of war, and with the perfection of firearms war became even more deadly.

With the introduction of aviation, making it possible to damage an entire country, of submarines that could strike merchant and military ships wherever they were, of long-range weapons that could strike from great distance, of armored tanks that could penetrate rapidly and deeply into lines of defense, war again and again underwent profound change. By this time whole countries and entire populations were involved. In fact, combatants and noncombatants can become targets of war: either because they are near military targets; or because the enemy wishes to break a country's will to resist by carpet-bombing; or because "military" and "civilian" targets can't always be distinguished; or, finally, because even the truly "civilian" targets could be considered "military" since they help to maintain the resistance and the fighting capacity of the adversary.

In this way war, which previously was "local" and "partial," has increasingly become "total" in a threefold sense. First, it involves whole nations, entire populations, all the cultural, artistic and religious wealth, and the economic riches of a country. Second, it involves not only two nations or a single group of nations, but many nations and ultimately the whole world. And, finally, it uses weapons of "total" and "indiscriminate" destruction.

The first example of "total" war was World War I; but it was actually World War II that fully assumed the character of "total" war. Not only did it involve almost all the nations of the world, the destruction of entire nations and the physical elimination of millions of people, it also made use of weapons of massive destruction, both in the practice of carpet-bombing to destroy an entire city by razing it to the ground—as happened in the bombing of Dresden (Feb. 13-14, 1944)—and above all in the dropping of the two atomic bombs on Hiroshima (Aug. 6, 1945) and on Nagasaki (Aug. 9, 1945).

In fact, on Aug. 6, 1945, humanity entered a new period of history radically different from the past: that of "total warfare." With the enormous development that has taken place between 1945 and today in thermonuclear, bacteriological and chemical weapons, the term "total warfare" has taken on a much more sinister meaning than in the past. If World War II was "total," with its casualty list of more than 50 million dead, most of them civilians, and the huge destruction of property of every sort, how much more "total" would war be today, fought as it would be with thermonuclear weapons? In the very first hours there would be hundreds of millions dead and in addition the destruction of every form of life throughout a large part of the planet.

But even if it does not reach the point of the deployment of thermonuclear or chemical weapons, modern warfare is always "total," to some extent. The Gulf War is a clear example. In that war thermonuclear weapons were not used, though at times the employment of tactical nuclear weapons was considered, and it was feared that the Iraqis might have recourse to chemical weapons. But the weapons used were so terribly destructive and lethal that—according to reliable sources—some 175,000 soldiers and 30,000 Iraqi civilians were killed and almost all of Iraq's civilian infrastructure (roads, bridges, irrigation systems) as well as its economic and industrial complex was destroyed. According to a United Nations representative, Iraq has been driven back into a preindustrial era. Unquestionably, a dramatic change—indeed a radical reversal—in the very nature of war is taking place. In other words, "modern" warfare is radically different from war in the past. This fact, as "Gaudium et Spes" (No. 80), rightly affirms "force(s) us to undertake a completely fresh reappraisal of war with an entirely new mentality (mente omnino nova)."

What is the meaning of this "completely fresh reappraisal" of which the council speaks? Evidently it means that today the Christian conscience must deal with the problem of war in a manner radically different from the past. To this end, it is helpful to understand how the church dealt with this problem in past centuries. In tracing very briefly the history of the church's relationship to war, we shall distinguish the practical approach that the church has taken toward war down through the centuries from the doctrinal formulations by which Catholic theologians, philosophers and jurists have attempted, without much success but with laudable intent, to place limits and restrictions on the phenomenon of war.

As for the practical approach, it has differed with different historical periods. During the period of persecutions (the first through fourth centuries), opposition to war and military service prevailed, and they were seen as incompatible with the spirit of the Gospel. Origen writes (*Contra Celsum*, V, 33): "We do not brandish the sword against anyone, neither do we learn to wage war, because we have become children of peace through Jesus, whom we follow as our leader." Nonetheless, there were Christians in the imperial army who saw no incompatibility between their faith and military service. People in the church held views of varying leniency or severity regarding them. Hippolytus of Rome (second and third centuries), for example, expressed the church's position this way: "The soldier in the ranks should not kill anyone. If he receives the order to do so, he should not follow it; nor should he take the military oath. If he acts otherwise, he is to be excommunicated (reiciatur). Catechumens or members of the faithful who wish to become soldiers are to be excommunicated, because they have despised God" (*La Tradizione Apostolica*, 16).

A profound change in the church's attitude toward the army and military service took place in the fourth and fifth centuries with the Christianization of the Roman Empire. Christians were obliged, under penalty of excommunication, to do military service; and with the law of Dec. 7, 415, of Theodosius II, pagans were not allowed to belong to the army. Thus by law the army was made up only of Catholics. Behind this profound change lay a new Christian view. Having but recently recovered from the terrible persecution of Diocletian, Christians saw the Christian Empire as a realization of the Messianic kingdom and the Christian emperor as a lieutenant of Christ. His wars could not but be considered "holy" or directed toward salvation. Furthermore, invasions from the north and east by "barbarians," pagans and Arian heretics like the Goths already threatened the Catholic Empire. There was, for instance, the terrible trauma of Alaric's sacking of Rome in 410. Catholics, therefore, felt compelled to fight for the empire's defense. Thus it was that the church accepted the army and war, but only as regrettable "necessities" due to "the wickedness of injustice," because "the wicked see war as a joy, while the good see it only as a necessity (belligerare malis videtur felicitas, bonis necessitas)" (St. Augustine, *De Civ. Dei, IV*, 15).

During premedieval times and in the Middle Ages themselves, the attitude of the church changed again. On the one hand, in a society that had now become great, the church spoke out against wars that would pit leaders and Christian states against one another. Not only did Nicholas I (d. 867) denounce war as "always satanic in its origins," but the Council of Narbonne (1045) declared: "A Christian who kills another Christian sheds the blood of Christ."

The church tried, therefore, to prevent war among Christians by offering to arbitrate disputes. Popes Paschal II, Gregory VII and Innocent III were able to do so successfully. Indeed Innocent III solemnly affirmed that the pope was God's sovereign mediator on earth. Above all the church tried to limit the times of combat by imposing the "truce of God," which prohibited fighting on certain days of the week (from Wednesday to Monday morning) and at certain times of the year (from Advent to Epiphany and from Ash Wednesday to the octave of Easter) and on feast days of Jesus, of the mother of God, of the apostles, of St. Lawrence, of St. Michael and the principal patron saints as well as days of fast and vigils (cf. *Decretale of Gregory*, Bk. 1, Ch. XXXIV, "De Tregua et Pace"). Furthermore, the church established norms for the protection of persons not involved in war and for the inviolability of certain places which functioned as sanctuaries for noncombatants. In fact, the church considered as its proper "ministry" (Gregory IV) the preservation of peace among Christians.

On the other hand, however, the church considered war "against enemies of the faith" as not only just but also "meritorious." Therefore the church obliged people to go on the Crusades, which were seen as a "work of Jesus Christ," for whose success all Christians must collaborate. Once a Crusade was begun, Christian rulers had to stop waging war on one another for four years and join the Crusade "to deliver the Holy Land from the hands of the impious" (Lateran Council IV, Const. 71, Dec. 14, 1215).

In the religious wars of the 16th and 17th centuries, the church was on the side of the Catholic states that fought against Protestant states and leaders. But, as political interests gradually took over in the wars among European states, the church seemed to distance herself from war, tending increasingly to set herself in opposition to it. Still it was not until the recent pontificates—from Benedict XV to John Paul II—that the church's opposition to war became absolute.

If we move now from the practical attitude taken toward war to a consideration of Catholic doctrine on the problem of war, we find that for many centuries theology accepted the theory of the "just war"—though it never became "official," in the sense of being sanctioned by the magisterium of the church. This theory starts from the presupposition that war is not per se and always immoral: For while war is always a misfortune and brings with it huge and terrible evils, there are circumstances in which it is necessary. There are, therefore, "just wars" (iusta bella) and "unjust wars." St. Augustine states that war is "just," if it is waged to avenge injustices (ad ulciscendum iniurias), that is, to restore rights that have been violated. War is unjust if it is waged with the "desire to inflict harm" (nocendi cupiditas) or with a "thirst for power" (libido dominandi) or to "enlarge one's territory" (regni cupiditas) or in order to obtain wealth and acquire glory. Fought for these motives, war is an "act of plunder on a grand scale" (grande latrocinium) (De. Civ. Dei, IV, 6).

Augustine's doctrine of the "just war" became the common heritage of medieval theology, which specified with increasing clarity the conditions necessary for a just war. Thus Gratian in his *Decretum* (p. II, c. XXIII, q. 2, c. 1) set down the conditions that would make a war "just": It must be declared by the competent authority (ex edicto geritur) and must be carried out in order to recover a nation's own possessions (de rebus repetendis) or to ward off an enemy's aggression (propulsandorum hostium causa). In turn, St. Thomas pointed out three conditions for a just war: 1) the authority of the ruler (auctoritas principis), since it is the ruler's duty to defend the state from internal disturbers of the peace as much as from external enemies; 2) a just cause (causa iusti), which means that those against whom war is being waged deserve to be opposed because of some fault on their part (propter aliquam culpam); 3) a right intention in fighting the war (intentio bellantium recta), namely, that the war is waged with the intention of promoting good or avoiding evil. If there is a just cause for war but the right intention is lacking—that is, if the motive for war is harm for the adversary, thirst for power or greed for wealth or if the war is fought with cruelty and a spirit of revenge (ulciscendi crudelitas)—such a war would be illicit (*Summa Theol.*, II-II, q. 40, a. 1, c). The sign of right intention is the search for peace, for "those who wage just wars do so because their intention is peace" (ivi, ad 3).

The doctrine of the "just war" was taken up by the theologians and jurists of the 16th and 17th centuries (F. de Vitoria, F. Suarez and L. Molina), but with a fundamental difference: The "just war" becomes the "right of war." Thus the doctrine moved from the "moral" sphere (bellum iustum) to the "juridical" (ius belli). What accounts for this change in perspective is the birth in the last centuries of the Middle Ages of national states. The essential characteristic of the national state—or, better, the "modern state"—is sovereignty. That is to say, the modern state does not recognize any power superior to itself, and it considers itself the only judge of its own interests and rights. Thus, if it maintains that its right has been violated by another state or that it must validate certain rights as its own (and it is the sole judge of this), then it has the ius belli, that is to say, the right to wage war against another state if it thinks that war is the best way of defending or vindicating its own sovereign rights. Clearly this theory of the ius belli is bound to lead to lasting conflicts among states. Catholic theologians and jurists accepted the principle of state "sovereignty" and hence the state's "right to wage war," but they tried to limit and control such a right with the theory of the "just war."

According to Francisco de Vitoria, the right of war is present when the war is just; and there are three reasons that make a war just. The first is the defense of what one owns, the recovery of goods taken unjustly and reparation for damages done. The second is the punishment of the culprit, that is, the one who, by violating the right of another, has committed a fault that merits punishment. For when order is violated, reparation is required. However, the violation must be so "definite, serious and persistent" that there is no other way of handling the situation that will bring about justice and achieve the right of the one wronged. The third is legitimate defense against an unjust aggressor, because "it is licit to repel violence with force (vim vi repellere licet)."

To these three causes for a just war, Francisco de Victoria adds two essential correctives. First and foremost, there must be a proportion between the gravity of the injustice that has been inflicted (or is on the point of being inflicted) and the evil consequences that will follow from the war. "When huge evils succeed war, such a war cannot be just" (*De Jure Belli*, 33, J. Boyer, Lyons, 1557, 405). Second, "if the war is useful for a particular province or state, but causes harm to the whole world or to Christianity, then it becomes an unjust war" (*De Potestate Civili*, 13, ivi, 193). This theory of the "just war" has become a "classical" position in Catholic theology and can be found in the manuals of philosophy and moral theology.

What can be said about this theory of the "just war"? Before all else, we have to realize that it was not intended to "justify" war, but rather to limit its frequency and cruelty by assigning conditions and very precise and strict rules that must be fulfilled before a war can be defined as "just." The intentions of Catholic theologians and jurists in elaborating the theory of the "just war" were therefore praiseworthy. But the theory has a serious flaw: Its conditions are unattainable; a war cannot really be conducted according to the criteria required for a just war. Indeed, a war may be waged for a "just motive" and therefore be a just war; but for it not to become "unjust," it must not produce "huge evils," it must not "cause damage to the whole world," it must not be conducted with cruelty and it must not inflict on the enemy damages that are more severe than the good results whose attainment would otherwise make the war a "just war." Clearly, these conditions for a "just war" were and are unattainable, because per sua natura war is waged with brutality; it always produces harm that far exceeds any advantages that may accrue in terms of justice and right; and it tends to inflict on the enemy much more serious damage than the good which is being sought and which would otherwise make the war "just." Actually war has its own proper "logic," which is to inflict on the enemy very serious harm, so much greater than what is probably necessary to achieve the end for which the war is being waged. The reason for this ferocity, which is peculiar to war, is the unwillingness to be satisfied with simply achieving the end for which the war was declared; the reason for war's ferocity is a desire to destroy the adversary in such a way that the adversary will be unable to recover and thus no longer constitute a threat in the future.

This explains the course of the Gulf War: Fought for a "just" motive—the liberation of Kuwait from the Iraqi invasion—by its own inexorable inner logic the war first brought about the systematic destruction of Iraq, on which were dropped, according to reports, as many as 90,000 tons of bombs, killing or wounding incalculable numbers of civilians; then it brought about the destruction of the Iraqi army so that Iraq would be unable to constitute a military threat in the future. In this way, the liberation of Kuwait caused the destruction of a country and the deaths of hundreds of thousands of people. At this point can anyone speak any longer of a "just war"? Or do we not rather have to say a "just war" is impossible because, even when a just cause is present, the wrongs that wars produce by their very nature are so grave and dreadful that they can never be justified in the light of conscience? This is all the more true because wars are neither necessary nor inevitable, since the injustices which they seek to remedy can be rectified by other means no less effective than war. Indeed, it is not true that war is the extrema ratio (last resort), because there are always peaceful ways to settle conflicts, provided one has the will and the patience to use them. In reality, to declare that war is the extrema ratio is often an attempt to justify the very desire to wage war. But what is an even more serious problem with the "just war" theory is that the "just cause" is used most of the time to give a moral and juridical guise to a war one intends to wage for purposes quite different from those that have been officially stated.

This shows that the theory of the "just war" is untenable and needs to be abandoned. With the single exception of a war of pure defense against an aggression actually taking place, one can say that "just wars" do not exist and that there is no "right to (wage) war." The "right of legitimate defense" is admitted by Pius XII as well as by the Second Vatican Council, at least in certain circumstances and in the absence of an international authority able to bring about a peaceful settlement of conflicts:

"Since human liberty is capable of unleashing an unjust conflict that may bring damages to a particular nation, it is certain that that nation can, under certain clearly defined conditions, resort to arms to defend itself" (Pius XII, *Discorsi e Radiomessaggi*, Vatican Polyglot Press, Vol. XX, Rome 1959, 173).

"War," the council states, "has not ceased to be part of the human scene. As long as the danger of war persists and there is no international authority with the necessary competence and power, governments cannot be denied the right of lawful self-defense (ius legitimae defensionis), once all peaceful efforts have failed" (*Gaudium et Spes*, 79).

We must once again, however, raise the issue that a war of lawful self-defense can become unlawful "when the damages that would come from such a war outweigh the evils that would come from tolerating the injustice in question;" in such a case "one would be obliged to submit to the injustice" (Pius XII, ibid., Vol. XV, 1954, 422). Moreover, even in a war of lawful self-defense, weapons of total destruction may not be used, especially such weapons as would elude human control and thus not meet the strict requirements of self-defense. The use of such weapons must be rejected "as immoral" because "in such a situation we are no longer dealing with a matter of 'defense' " against injustice and the necessary "safeguarding" of lawful possessions, but with the "annihilation, pure and simple, of all human life within a given radius of action. This is not permitted under any title" (ibid., XVI, 1955, 169).

But what has definitively put the theory of the "just war" in crisis—and even the war of lawful self-defense, as Pius XII has observed—is the advent of "modern warfare," which per sua natura allows the use of weapons of mass destruction, weapons that elude human control. Whereas past wars were fought with weapons that caused limited damage and were controllable, modern warfare is fought with weapons of mass destruction that elude human control. This means that both soldiers and civilians are killed or wounded—it is illusory to speak of military operations as "surgical operations"!— and purely civilian as well as military targets are destroyed (even when the intention may not be so much to strike at civilian populations and targets as it is to demoralize the enemy).

Besides, "modern warfare" cannot be limited in the damage it causes, but entails practically the "total" destruction of a country. It can even involve the disastrous slaughter of civilians. Think of the destruction of Hamburg and Dresden and the dropping of the two atomic bombs on Hiroshima and Nagasaki—considered necessary to break the will of the enemy who began the war and who bloodied their hands with horrible crimes. Truly, modern warfare unleashes a violence that, given the use of modern weapons, has no limits.

What has already been said is likewise valid even in cases where only so-called conventional weapons are used. For, as we have seen in the Gulf War, because of technological advances these weapons have reached a point where they have enormous destructive power: Think of the white phosphorous bombs used against Iraqi soldiers in flight from Kuwait. And, modern warfare entails recourse to thermonuclear, chemical and bacteriological weapons or, at the very least, there is always the risk they will be used. Since, as the Second Vatican Council says, "every act of war directed to the indiscriminate destruction of whole cities or vast areas with their inhabitants is a crime against God and humanity itself (est crimen contra Deum et ipsum hominem), which merits firm and unequivocal condemnation," and since "hazards peculiar to modern warfare (belli hodierni) consist in

145

the fact that they expose those possessing recently developed weapons to the risk of perpetrating crimes like these and, by an inexorable chain of events (connexione quadam inexorabili) of urging humanity to even worse acts of atrocity" (*Gaudium et Spes*, 80), we can only conclude that modern warfare is always immoral.

Besides being immoral, warfare today is useless and harmful. On the one hand, it does not solve, even apparently and momentarily, the problems it has unleashed. John XXIII affirmed in *Pacem in Terris* (No. 127) that "in our age, which boasts of its atomic power, it is irrational to think that war is a suitable instrument for redressing the violation of rights (alienum est a ratione bellum iam aptum esse ad violata iura sarcienda)." On the other hand, not only does it not solve problems, it aggravates them, rendering a solution practically impossible and in fact creating yet more grievous problems. Thus it sows the seeds of future conflicts and wars. Moreover, since the "peace" that concludes a war is violently imposed by the victor on the vanquished, engendering in them feelings of revenge, the very peace itself becomes the seed of new wars. Thus the seed of World War II was the "peace" of Versailles, which ended World War I.

In fact, war almost never ends with a true peace: It always leaves behind a remnant of hatred and a thirst for revenge that will explode as soon as the opportunity arises. That is why human history has been an unending series of wars. War initiates a spiral of hatred and violence that is extremely difficult to stop.

War is therefore useless, since it solves no problems, and damaging because it aggravates problems and makes them insoluble. However one puts it, the Gulf War shows this to be true. Certainly Kuwait has been liberated and international law re-established, but at what price and with what kind of results? The price paid has been the destruction of the invading country (Iraq) and the economic ruin of the invaded country (Kuwait). According to *The Economist*, 120 trillion lire will be needed for their reconstruction. Further results were the massacre of Palestinians (and, it is understood, of Iraqis) in Kuwait by the emir, Al-Sabah, when he returned. The civil war in Iraq led to the slaughter of many Kurds and Shiites. Pollution affected an enormous expanse of the Persian Gulf, not to mention the immense military cost of the war, calculated by the U.S. Congressional Budget Office at 230.2 trillion lire. There is also the fact that not one of the very serious problems of the Middle East—that of the Palestinians, the Lebanese and the Kurds—which after the war's end seemed to be approaching an easy and immediate solution—has been resolved; on the contrary, these and other problems engendered by the war have been aggravated and their solution seems even more difficult. Therefore, it seems clear that this war was not only immoral but also irrational, because it proved useless and produced further disasters.

The experience of the Gulf War explains the position that the church in the 20th century has taken toward war, expressed in an absolute condemnation of war and an effort to come to grips with problematic issues of the past, namely, the "just war" and the "holy war" in defense of the faith. The church's position shows a development of the Christian conscience regarding the absolute immorality of war. Thus in four important documents the church has formally condemned war: on May 23, 1920, with Benedict XV's encyclical *Pacem Dei Munus*; on April 11, 1963, with John XXIII's encyclical *Pacem in Terris*; on Dec. 7, 1965, with the pastoral constitution *Gaudium et Spes*; and on May 1, 1991, with John Paul II's encyclical *Centesimus Annus*:

> "No, never again war, which destroys the lives of innocent peo-
> ple, teaches how to kill, throws into upheaval even the lives of
> those who do the killing and leaves behind a trail of resentment
> and hatred, thus making it all the more difficult to find a just
> solution of the very problems which provoked the war. Just as

the time has finally come when in individual states a system of private vendetta and reprisal has given way to the rule of law, so too a similar step forward is now urgently needed in the international community (No. 52)."

But in the very act of condemning war, the church affirms that "peace is possible." It is "neither a dream nor a utopia" and indeed today it is essential "to move resolutely toward the absolute prohibition of war" (John Paul II). Humanity is not, then, condemned to the "inevitability" of war but can free itself from its "necessity" or better, its "shackles."

There is, however, a more important and more basic reason that impels the church not only to condemn war, but to make herself a promoter of peace. She must announce the Gospel, which is a "Gospel of peace." This means that the proclamation and promotion of peace among people is part of her religious mission. Therefore, when the church speaks of the need to involve herself in the cause of peace and declares herself against war, she is not invading the field of politics, but is staying within the sphere of her own proper religious and moral mission. So much is this so that if she failed to do it, the church would be unfaithful to the Gospel of Jesus, which proclaims as "blessed" those who are "peacemakers," for "they will be called children of God" (Matthew 5:9). Indeed, through Jesus men and women are brothers and sisters of one another because they are children of God in heaven. This means that they must rid themselves of the categories of "stranger" and "enemy," categories so basic to the ideology of war. The church, in whatever she does, seeks only to drive home the Gospel's call to brotherhood and sisterhood among people.

The church, therefore, condemns war and wants peace. But what does it mean for the church today "to oppose war" and "to want peace?" "To oppose war" means to oppose "the ideology of war." In practical terms it means opposing the idea that war is able to resolve the problems at the root of conflicts. It means opposing the idea of war as the extrema ratio, because in practice there is no extrema ratio, as it is impossible to prove that all the means to avoid war were considered and put into action. In addition, the one who decides that there is no alternative to war is the very person with a vested interest in waging it and who has already decided to do so and is simply waiting for a suitable time to begin. Being against war and for peace also means opposing the idea that war is "necessary" or "inevitable," and that peace is not "possible." Finally, it means opposing the idea that wars are waged for noble motives: to restore a universal order of justice and peace or simply to make amends for injustices. For at most these noble motives—which some people do not lack—in most cases provide a juridical and moral cover for the true reasons for war: political domination and economic interest. In other words, to oppose the "ideology of war" means to do what is needed to unmask war by showing it as it really is by uncovering its motives and its results, by demonstrating that it is always the poor and the weak who pay for war, whether they wear a military uniform or belong to the civilian population.

But the church cannot be content with condemning war. She must want peace. But what kind of peace? Not a peace founded on injustice or violence or terror or mutual mistrust, but a peace founded on justice, solidarity and mutual trust. The church maintains that there can be no peace where situations of grave injustice persist and where the just aspirations of people—for freedom, for self-determination, for a homeland of their own, for the right to live a life worthy of human dignity—are frustrated by force and violence. There can be no peace where feelings of frustration and hatred and vengeance are fostered among peoples and nations and continents. There can be no peace where mutual trust is absent and peace is based on "a balance of terror" sustained by an ongoing arms race, whether the arms are conventional or thermonuclear. That is why the church—decisively proclaiming herself for peace and against any war—asks that remedies be found for situations of injustice that exist in today's world and that otherwise will be the forerunners of new wars. Above all, solutions must be found for the fundamental injustice that has created dramatic conditions of growing poverty in the southern half of the planet.

This situation cannot be changed unless, among other things, we place a limit on arms production, the cost of which is mind-boggling. To mention only some of the weapons systems used in the Gulf War, a Tomahawk missile cost 1.5 billion lire; the Patriot anti-ballistic missile, 1.2 billion lire; the F-14 Tomcat fighter plane, 60 billion lire; a Tornado fighter plane, 70 billion lire; an AWACS radar plane, 121 billion lire; the radar-evading F-117 Stealth fighter plane, 130 billion lire; an Apache helicopter, 12 billion lire; an Abrams M-1 tank, 5 billion lire; and a Challenger tank, 10 billion lire. It is a question of wasting immense wealth that could—and should—be used to eliminate the poverty of the millions of people dying of hunger.

It is also necessary to heal situations of local injustice, some of which are particularly explosive, such as the situation of Lebanon, of the Palestinians, of the Kurds, of the Cypriots and also the problem of the security of the state of Israel. Last March 4, John Paul II, opening the meeting in the Vatican of the Catholic patriarchs and the presidents of the episcopal conferences of the countries involved in the crisis of the Gulf, recalled that "peace and justice walk together," and that there will be a "just and lasting" peace in the Middle East only if the problems of that region are resolved: an effective respect for the principle of the territorial integrity of the countries involved; a solution to the Lebanese and Palestinian problems; regulation of the arms traffic; and reaching an agreement on disarmament of the region. As a matter of fact, peace in the Middle East has not at all been restored by the allies' victory over Iraq. It must be built patiently through negotiations that satisfy all just demands of the people of the area. It must be a peace based on justice, solidarity and mutual trust that will eliminate political and social oppression as well as all types of imperialism and exploitation. To build such a peace is an immense undertaking, but it is the only way to ensure that the Gulf War is not just the beginning of an endless series of horrors.

About Pax Christi USA

Pax Christi USA is the national Catholic peace movement. Its 14,000 members work for the transformation of society through nonviolence and advocate peacemaking as a priority in the Catholic Church in the United States. The movement, headquartered in Erie, Pennsylvania, publishes peace education literature and develops ministry programs that promote justice for the sake of creating a more peaceful, just and sustainable world. Pax Christi USA is a section of Pax Christi International, which is active in more than 30 countries. Our membership includes over 550 religious communities; over 450 parish sponsors; over 140 bishops; over 130 Youth & Young Adult Forum members; approximately 230 Pax Christi local groups; and 18 regions that coordinate activities in their geographic areas.

The work of Pax Christi USA begins in personal life and extends to communities of reflection and action to transform structures of society. Pax Christi USA rejects war and every form of violence and domination. It advocates primacy of conscience, economic and social justice and respect for all creation.

Membership is open to all who support Pax Christi USA's statement of purpose. Regular membership is $35 per year, entitling the subscriber to Pax Christi USA's quarterly publication, the *Catholic Peace Voice*, and regular membership mailings. Full membership benefits are extended to those living on limited incomes who cannot afford the entire membership fee. For information about joining Pax Christi USA or to receive a catalogue of our publications, please call, write, e-mail or contact us via our web site.

Pax Christi USA
532 West Eighth St.
Erie, PA 16502
814.453.4955
info@paxchristiusa.org
www.nonviolence.org/pcusa